I Believe

The Thirteen Principals of Faith
A Confirmation Textbook

I Believe

The Thirteen Principals of Faith
A Confirmation Textbook

by

Rabbi Kerry M. Olitzky
and
Rabbi Ronald H. Isaacs

KTAV Publishing House, Inc.
Hoboken, New Jersey

ISBN 0-88125-627-7

Distributed by
KTAV Publishing House, Inc.
900 Jefferson Street
Hoboken, N.J. 07030

Manufactured in the
United States of America

Contents

An Introduction to Jewish Belief

Most of us would like to be able to state what we believe, as well as to articulate the basic principles of Judaism in a few sentences—especially when we are asked questions about our religious beliefs and the Jewish tradition by others. But it just isn't that easy. If someone were to make a list of statements about Judaism for us to memorize, and then repeat them word for word to others (that's what religious educators call a catechism), this method would rob us of the opportunity to struggle with Jewish belief and arrive at a decision about personal faith on our own. Nevertheless, scholars throughout history have tried to communicate the basic concepts of Judaism in just a few words or sentences. This book is built around one such attempt—perhaps the most famous and most familiar—developed by one of the greatest Jewish philosophers and theologians of all time: Moses Maimonides. You may have also heard him simply called by the acronym Rambam or by his full name, Moses ben Maimon. By studying what Maimonides had to say about Jewish belief, using it as a prism through which to look at the entire landscape of Jewish faith, we are able to reach an understanding about what we personally believe as Jews.

This is not an easy book. If you take this work seriously, it will not be an easy year either. We want to tell you that at the very outset of our work together. The exercises in this book will force you to think for yourselves. They will make you rethink some of the things you may have been taught in religious school—or even by your parents—and have taken for granted, without really questioning, probing, analyzing, or trying to get a sense of the truth of a particular idea.

At the conclusion of this book, we think that you will be able to comfortably and competently say "This is what I believe . . . ", and then proceed to explain what you believe and where those beliefs fit into (or, alternatively, do not fit into) a primary system of Jewish belief. Through this book, you will learn that there is a mainstream of belief in Judaism: the principles that have been accepted historically by the majority of Jews. However, you will also encounter many beliefs that are held by those who may be considered "on the fringe," with which you may agree. That's okay. Not everyone agrees about which principles are indispensable to Judaism. There is flexibility in Jewish thought; there are some choices to be made. There is an old joke, "Ask two Jews; get three opinions." That's what makes Judaism such a colorful religious tradition—and makes us all want to be part of it. The historian Michael Meyer imagines Judaism as a twisted rope within which threads are weaving in and out throughout its history. The various strands give strength to the rope. Some form the core of Judaism, providing it with its durability. Other strands weave in and out. And there are yet others that remain on the outside, subject to fraying. These eventually break off and fall away.

Now, it is also possible that at the end of this book you may reject some of the beliefs that other Jews, especially a parent or grandparent, may hold sacred. We understand that challenge. It is part of the risk of an honest and open dialogue with our past. We have faced it ourselves at various times in our lives. Don't beat yourself up about it. We have to find a way to embrace that difficulty. As rabbis, we have learned that Jewish belief is not as much about "knowing truth" as it is about "struggling toward the truth." Menachem Mendl of Kotzk, a Hasidic rabbi whose words you will find scattered throughout this book and elsewhere, had a zealous passion for truth, which he sought his entire life. Like him, we know that one does not wake up one morning and simply believe. Jewish belief is a lifelong struggle. Thus, Confirmation is more about committing to the struggle to believe than about committing to any one particular system of Jewish belief. In his Memoirs: *All the Rivers Run to It*, Elie Wiesel, the noted author and Nobel laureate, who writes as a witness to the Shoah, retells an insightful story (which was, in turn, told to him by the "young" Rebbe of

Wishnitz). This story helps us to understand. He writes, "The great Rebbe Nachman of Bratzlav tells the story of a child lost in the forest. Gripped by panic, he cries, 'Father, father, save me!' As long as he cries, he can hope that his father will hear him. If he stops, he is lost." It's the same thing with us: As long as we cry out in search of God, we are not lost on our journey, and our search for understanding and ultimate meaning. When we stop looking—or stop crying out (as the Nachman of Bratzlav story styles it)—that's when we get lost along the way.

A Word About Confirmation

It is not coincidental that we chose the topic of faith and religious belief as the primary text for your year of Confirmation studies. After all, Confirmation is all about standing in front of your family and community, and publicly declaring your beliefs; in other words, *confirming* your faith. Hence, the word Confirmation. The Confirmation ceremony generally takes place in connection with Shavuot, when the Israelites stood at the foot of Mount Sinai and God revealed the Torah to them—and, indirectly, to us. The rabbis of the Midrash suggest that God spoke to the people in 600,000 voices—one for each Israelite who stood at the foot of the mountain—so that we might all understand the message of Torah. Imagine the scene for a moment. Clouds surrounded the mountain. Thunder and lightning. The revelation. Each time we read the Torah aloud publicly, we are reenacting that scene. It is that event which has led us—and all the others who came before us in the meandering course of the history of the Jewish people—to the day of your Confirmation.

Getting Started

No matter what you believe about God, even if you have taken the time to really think about what you believe, it may be difficult to talk to others about that belief. Before we consider any one individual belief about God and Judaism, this exercise may help you get comfortable with talking about it at all. Begin with the phrase, "I believe _____." Then make a list of things that you believe to be true about the world in general, your family, your neighborhood (even your dog, cat, or bird, if you have one). Just to help you get started, here is a short list of different kinds of things we believe:

1. We believe that just as the night follows day, day follows night.

2. We believe that plant life regenerates through the cycle of the seasons.

3. We believe that it is possible to overcome hate through love.

4. We believe that the force of gravity causes things to fall toward the ground.

5. We believe that the New York Rangers will win the Stanley Cup this year (okay, maybe not).

Now it's your turn:
1.
2.
3.
4.
5.

Do others in your family or your circle of friends share these beliefs? Are you committed to them, or if others prove that they are wrong, are you prepared to give them up? These are the hard questions of belief that we have to consider.

What is belief all about anyway? Ask a parent or friend to try to define it. Then, discuss it with a few people. See if people of different ages have a different perspective on it. Then, look up the word in the dictionary. Does it apply to the things that you listed above? Or is belief tied to more significant, life-changing things? In your own words, try to define "belief" here.

Belief:

_____

_____

What We Believe

Confirmation is about a special kind of belief: religious belief. It is not really about God (although for us, as Jews, belief in God will be a primary component of it). And we might as well say it up front. We assert that belief in God is the foundation of all belief. Jewish belief is also about what some people call "the really important stuff" in life, things that have lasting and important value. We contend that Judaism provides us with answers to those really important questions. We think that you will feel the same way—at the end of your study toward Confirmation (and beyond).

But Confirmation is also about our relationship to the world. With all the many new things we are learning about the world and about ourselves, it takes time to sort out what we believe from what we don't believe. We have been taught some things that seem to conflict with our experience of the world. And there are other things about the world which we have been forced to learn on our own. There are still other things that we may have been taught as young children, because our parents and teachers thought that we were too young to learn the truth. (Remember the baby-delivering stork story?) So now that we are young adults, what do we do?

As young Jewish adults, we seek ways to confirm what we believe to be true about our religious world. Our goal is to help you explore these concepts, and to arrange them in such a way in your mind that you can review them periodically and then, if you choose to do so, share them with others.

Before we go any further, we have to remember that Judaism differs from other religions. Thus, Jewish belief differs from other systems of belief as well. Some of these differences are major, others are minor. Some people may try to tell you that it does not matter what you believe, that the only important thing is to be a good human being—what our grandparents meant when they said, "Be a *mensch."* Hillel said it this way, "In a place where no one is acting right, strive to be human" (Pirke Avot 2:6). But there is more to life than just being a decent human being. Judaism has a particular system of belief, one that is specifically designed to bring the messianic age, a perfection of the world.

Since you are participating in this course for Confirmation, either you have been born into Judaism or made the choice—with other members of your family—to join the Jewish people. Thus, the Jewish belief system is ours. For right now, that is enough to make it special. Through this course in Confirmation, you will learn some of what makes Jewish belief and Judaism special, beyond the simple fact that it forms the basis of our heritage.

How Judaism Differs

Rabbi Abba Hillel Silver, who was a confidant of President Franklin D. Roosevelt, once wrote a book called *Where Judaism Differs.* In this book, he describes how Judaism differs from Christianity. But we also have to consider how it differs from the other religions. Thus, some of the exercises in this book will help you see Judaism and Jewish belief more clearly as it is distinguished from other faiths. Judaism is focused on a life of faith which is understood in the context of action. That's why the statement *Na'aseh v'nishmah* ("We will act, and we will hearken," Exodus 24:7) is critical to Judaism. What we believe is actually seen through what we do with our lives, how we behave, how we act toward others.

Take a moment to think about how the life you lead may differ from the lives of friends who are not Jewish. Do you look at things the same way? How are your beliefs different? Have you ever talked with your friends about those beliefs?

Wishful thinking is different from faith. *Emunah*, the Hebrew word for "faith," may be expressed as a trust or a confidence—something on which we can always depend. Faith in Jewish tradition, faith in God, is understood as a means to help the individual lead a moral life. That's the purpose of having faith in the first place. When we respond to something by saying "amen," it is our way of affirming that belief, that is, we are willing to behave in such a way that reflects that belief statement.

Faith is not a free gift, something that is given to us. It must be constantly nurtured. It is a slow, rigorous process, and it requires self-discipline.

A Belief System

While no belief system is really perfect, any such system is designed to help you answer most, if not all, of the questions that individuals face as they confront life and the world. For example: Why is there evil in the world? Why do bad things happen to good people? Why was there a Shoah? Why do diseases take those we love? How does nature regenerate itself each year? Add your own questions below.

1.

2.

3.

4.

5.

You will get a chance to discuss some of these questions with your teacher (and/or your rabbi), as well as your classmates.

I Believe With Perfect Faith

Each statement in Maimonides' Thirteen Principles of Faith begins with the phrase "I believe with perfect faith." By stating it this way, Maimonides seems to imply that Judaism demands an absolute commitment from us. But Maimonides does not use the word "absolute." While we might expect it to be otherwise, Jewish faith is not void of doubt and question. It does not come to the individual automatically—even if one wants to believe. To be a believing Jew is to doubt, to question, to challenge. The Talmud records an incident in which Rabbis Hillel and Shammai disagree vehemently about a religious principle. In the end, both opinions are accepted.

One of our favorite Hasidic rabbis, Levi Yitzchak of Berditchev, was famous for his arguments with God. He was not prepared to simply accept what God dished out to him or the Jewish community he led. Instead, he would stand on the *bima* in his synagogue for hours demanding mercy and justice from God. We call this attitude or approach *chutzpah clappei malah*, or audacity toward Heaven.

Thus, we come to understand that "perfect" Jewish faith is one that is replete with imperfections, just like all of us. It seems contradictory, but that's Jewish religious logic.

Godtalk

Godtalk, as we like to call this kind of discussion, may not be a popular subject of conversation among your friends. The series of statements which starts each chapter and much of this book is about learning how to talk about God. It is also about opening oneself up to experience God in one's life, because it is difficult to talk about anything that one has not experienced. Such discussion is what Confirmation is all about. So let's begin by discussing your first religious (or holy) experience, that is, the first experience of God that you can recall. Write out as many of the details here. Don't worry about complete sentences or the correct spelling of words. Just get down as many of the details as possible.

_____

_____

_____

Have you ever talked about this experience with anyone? Have you ever thought about why you may not have wanted to talk to others about God? Think back over the past year. How many times have you or your family or your friends had a discussion about God? What words came up in the discussion that described your interaction with God? List them here.

_____

_____

_____

_____

What Can We Believe?

Some people think that given the amount of evil in the world—particularly since the Holocaust—including diseases and the many things that happen to people, it is nearly impossible to believe in anything that may remotely be considered God. But Judaism demands from us a balanced perspective. We have to look at both sides of everything: darkness and light. Death may be a high price to pay for living, but our world is constructed in such a way that one does not come without the other. Your own growth and maturation, seen as positive from everyone's perspective, also means that such growth will eventually evolve into old age and death, making room for those who will inherit the earth after you're gone. It is part of the cycle of life.

From Faith to Deeds

Judaism is not merely a religion of belief. It is also a religion of action. Some will even say that what one does is more important than what one believes. As the popular saying goes, "Actions speak louder than words."

The Spectrum of Jewish Belief: Reform, Conservative, and All the Rest

Some people think that Judaism works like a number line, as if you can mark all 613 *mitzvot* in a row and then plot the various religious movements along that line. According to this (ill-placed) logic, Reform would be on one end of the line of observance and Orthodoxy on the other. The big problem here is that such an approach does not take into consideration the process by which an individual came to believe. Thus, it is the ideology of a movement that guides them individually to make a decision about the practice and not the expression of one's religious practices that determines in which Jewish movement one belongs or should be placed. For example, personal autonomy is a foundational principle of Reform Judaism. Thus, an individual can make a personal decision about his or her own personal practices, provided that it is done through a process of study. Thus, such decisions are made on the basis of knowledge and information and not convenience or laziness. If a Reform Jew *chooses* to keep kosher, put on tefillin, and not drive on Shabbat, that individual is still a Reform Jew, because he or she has chosen to do so. On the other hand, if a Conservative Jew joins a Conservative synagogue, then he or she is bound by the decisions of that community as guidelines for personal religious life. And when the Law Committee of the Rabbinical Assembly makes a decision—which may include a liberal interpretation of Jewish law (such as driving on Shabbat but only to the synagogue), then the individual is obligated to abide by that decision as a member of the Conservative movement. For some people, these may seem like major issues (for others, they may be considered rather minor), but they are only used for illustrations here to help frame our study together. What matters to us is not the movement with which one affiliates. What matters to us is that you identify Jewishly, and begin to understand the beliefs implicit in that identification.

So where do you stand now? (Don't worry, you'll have a chance at the end of the book to consider the question once again.)

Moses Maimonides: A Brief Biography

Moses Maimonides was born on March 30, 1135, in Cordova, Spain. In rabbinical literature, he is also called RaMBaM—an acronym constructed from the name Rabbi Moses ben Maimon. In some contexts, he is also referred to as *Ha-nesher Ha-gadol* (the Mighty Eagle). Maimonides' father, Maimon ben Joseph, was the *dayyan*, or judge, of Cordova. He was a man of outstanding piety and scholarship who traced his ancestry to Rabbi Judah ha-Nasi, the compiler of the Mishnah. While little is known about Moses Maimonides' mother, legend suggests that Moses' father had a dream in which he was instructed to marry the daughter of a butcher who lived not far from Cordova. He took the dream seriously, and married the woman—who died in childbirth. Moses' father later remarried.

As is the case with many great scholars in our history—perhaps as a way of maintaining hope for children in our own midst who seem uninterested in study—a story is told that Moses was really indifferent about his study while he was a child. The older Maimonides was distressed about this attitude, and called Moses to his side, chiding him about where a life of ignorance might lead him, the shame it would bring to his family and to him. Following this upbraiding, Moses ran into the local synagogue, found a place to cower, and cried himself to sleep. When he awoke, he felt like a new person—and committed himself to the arduous task of study. The boy then went to the house of the celebrated Rabbi Joseph ibn Migash, who had previously served as a teacher to the elder Maimonides, and diligently applied himself to study. Similar legends hold that Maimonides later returned to his native city of Cordova while still a boy and went straight to that same synagogue to deliver a scholarly discourse, to surprise his father.

Cordova fell to the Almohads in 1148. As a result, thirteen-year-old Moses and his family had to flee the religious persecution that followed. Little is known about him during the ten years which followed, as his family wandered throughout Spain. However, it was during this period that Maimonides probably began his commentary to the Mishnah—and laid the foundation for much of the literary activity that occupied most of his adult life. During this period of turmoil in his life, he also wrote a short piece on the Jewish calendar (*Ma'amar ha-Ibbur*), an essay on logic (*Millot Higgayon*), and collected notes for his commentary to several tractates of the Talmud.

Then, in 1159/1160, the family settled in Fez, North Africa, where Maimonides studied under Rabbi Judah ha-Kohen ibn Susan. In Fez, Maimonides encountered many Jews who had converted to Islam. This troubled him. So he wrote a letter to them, *Iggeret ha-Nechamah* (Letter of Consolation), suggesting that their prayers and good works would still make them considered as Jews. This concern over the large number of converts also prompted him to write *Iggeret ha-Shemad* (Letter on Forced Conversion) and *Iggeret Kiddush ha-Shem* (Letter on the Sanctification of the Divine Name). These subsequent letters are not so tolerant as his previous efforts. Instead, he encourages people to emigrate rather than "transgress the divine law." He wrote,

> In former times, Israelites were called upon to transgress the law by acts. Now, however, we are not asked to render active homage to idolatry, but only to recite an empty formula which the Moslems themselves know we are uttering insincerely only to avoid the bigot. If ever under these circumstances, a Jew surrenders one's life for the sanctification of the Name of God before humans, he has done nobly well, and his reward is great before God. But if a person asks me, "Shall I be slain or utter the formula of Islam?"

I answer, "Utter the formula and live."

Many took Maimonides' advice seriously. His teacher, Judah ibn Susan, took his life. Moses and family fled Fez in 1165. They traveled to Israel, and eventually arrived in Acre (Akko). As was customary, the family of Maimonides celebrated these stops along their family journey, marking them as family festivals which they celebrated for many generations that followed.

Following a short residence in the land of Israel, where he visited many of its religious sites, he and his family moved to Egypt. Following a brief stay in Alexandria, they settled in Fostat (Old Cairo) in 1167. Moses' father died about the same time. Perhaps the presence of a Karaite majority in Cairo (and its implicit challenge to rabbinic authority) influenced him to locate there. Moses' brother, David, supported the family so that Moses could devote himself to study and writing. Thus, one year after settling in Fostat, Maimonides completed his commentary to the Mishnah (1168). Then, his brother David died, the result of drowning in the Indian Ocean while on a business trip. Stricken with grief, Maimonides was unable to function for an entire year. He refused to use his knowledge of the Jewish tradition in order to earn a livelihood. It was not until he was invited to become one of the physicians to al-Fadil, the vizier (appointed by Saladin, whom he succeeded as ruler of Egypt after Saladin departed in 1174). Due to his fame in that position, he was later named head of the Jewish community of Fostat (1177). And, in 1185, Moses was appointed chief physician to the vizier.

During these years in Fostat, Maimonides achieved an amazing level of literary output. He finished his *Sefer Mitzvot* (1170). He composed his well-known epistle to Yemenite Jewry (1172). This letter is a response to a letter addressed to him by Rabbi Jacob al-Fayumi which refers to the critical condition of the Jews in Yemen. In his reply, Maimonides attempts to prove that the sufferings of the Jews, together with the numerous instances of apostasy, were foretold by the prophets, especially by Daniel, and must not perplex the faithful. Attempts had been made in the past to do away with Judaism. They had invariably failed. The same would hold true for present attempts, for "religious persecutions are of but short duration."

In Egypt, he remarried—his first wife having died young. Abraham was born to the new couple, whom Moses personally educated. In addition, he devoted himself to his disciple Joseph ibn Sham'un (some suggest it was ibn Akhnin), for whom he prepared his *Guide for the Perplexed*. By 1180, Moses Maimonides had finished his *Mishneh Torah* (A Summary of the Torah), a work that took him ten years to complete for "his own benefit, to save him in his advanced age the trouble and necessity of consulting the Talmud on every occasion." This work was designed to be a religious guide based to revelation and tradition. The *Mishneh Torah* was also called *Yad ha-Chazaka*, or *The Strong Hand*.

He completed his *Guide for the Perplexed* in 1190/1191. In this very difficult philosophical work, composed in Arabic and written in Hebrew characters, he sought to provide a religious guide (like the *Mishneh Torah*) based on philosophy, rather than on revelation and tradition. The work was translated into Hebrew by Rabbi Samuel ibn Tibbon during Rambam's own lifetime (who was consulted on the difficulty of certain Hebrew passages). Maimonides dedicated the work to his disciple Joseph, who was disappointed, for he felt the work lacked a reconciliation of faith with science. A second translation was made by Judah Alharizi. The same year that the *Guide* was finished, Maimonides wrote to his student:

I inform you that I have acquired a very great reputation in medicine among the great, such as the Chief Qadi, the Princes, the House of Al-Fadil (his protector), and other grandees, from whom I do not obtain a large fee. As for the ordinary people, I am placed too high for them to reach me. This obliges me continually to waste my day in Cairo visiting the (noble) sick. When I return to Fostat, I am too tired for the rest of the day and night to pursue my study of medical books, which I need. For, you know, how long and difficult this art is for a conscientious and exact man who does not want to state anything which he cannot support by argument, and without knowing where it has been said, and how it can be demonstrated.

Only four years after completing the *Guide*, Maimonides prepared a treatise on resurrection (1195). In a letter to his friend, Rabbi Samuel ibn Tibbon in France, he wrote (1198):

> You will expose yourself in vain to the dangers of the journey, as you will not find a moment during the day or night to speak with me. The Sultan resides in Cairo, and I dwell in Fostat. The distance between the two places is a double Sabbath's day's journey (about a mile and a half). My duties to the Sultan are heavy. I must visit him early in the morning. If he feels weak, or any of his children or the inmates of his harem is ill, I cannot leave Cairo but must spend the greater part of my day in the palace. Also, if any of the officials falls ill, I have to attend to him, and I thus spend the whole day there. In brief, I repair to Cairo every day in the morning; and even if nothing unusual happens, I do not return to Fostat until the noon hour. Then I am fatigued and hungry, and I find the courts of my house full of people, prominent and common, gentlemen, theologians, and judges, waiting for my return. I dismount from my animal, wash my hands, go forth to them, and entreat them to wait for me while I take a slight refreshment, my only meal in twenty-four hours. After that, I attend to the patients, and prescribe for them. Patients go in and out until nightfall; or, I assure you, until two hours in the night. I talk to them lying on my back because of weakness. When the night falls, I feel so weak, I cannot speak any more. Thus no Jew can have a private discussion with me, except on the Sabbath.

Moses Maimonides died on December 13, 1204, at the age of seventy; he was buried in Tiberias, Israel. In Fostat, the Jewish community mourned for three days; in Jerusalem, they fasted. According to legend, as the funeral procession was going through the desert, it was attacked by a band of Bedouins. As soon as the robbers realized that they were about to desecrate Maimonides' body, they refrained from their assault, and instead hung their heads in shame. Forming a protective circle around the funeral cortege, they followed it all the way to the burial place in Palestine. For Maimuni, as they called him, was a man they all revered. Many times he had treated them for their illnesses without asking for pay for his services. And in Cairo, there is an old prayer house called the Synagogue of Maimonides. On the southern side, there is a small shrine in which an eternal light is kept burning in memory of Rambam. It is said that in this shrine his body remained an entire week before it was taken to its burial place. The folks in Jerusalem lamented, "the glory had departed from Israel; the ark of Adonai had been taken away."

PRINCIPLE ONE

The Creator God

I believe with perfect faith that the Creator, praised be Your name, is the Author and Guide of everything that has been created, and that God alone has made, does make, and will make all things.

Getting Started: Some Background

So where do we begin? With ourselves? With the creation of the world? With God?

Maimonides decided to begin by establishing a relationship among all three elements in his presentation of the basic principles of Judaism. What would be your first belief statement?

Some philosophers assert that all existence is composed of four basic elements. What do you think these elements are?

1. _____
2. _____
3. _____
4. _____

Perhaps Maimonides should have suggested that God was the Creator of these basic elements, and that everything else evolved from them. Why do you think that he did not begin that way?

If these thirteen principles represent the basic belief system of Judaism, then one would expect Maimonides to begin with the more important ideas. Write down what you consider to be the primary core belief in Judaism. How would you rephrase Maimonides' first statement about basic Jewish belief? Write your answer below.

_____

_____

_____

_____

_____

_____

Maimonides began with the self, the "I," and then establishes a relationship between the "I" (that's all of us) and God. Some mystics believe that in the relationship between the "I" and God, the "I" is actually merged into God. They call this *devekut*, or clinging (similar to the modern Hebrew word for glue, *devek*). The result is what is called the abdication of the ego or the self. Consider what Jacob said to himself, as reported in Genesis 28:16, after dreaming of a ladder to heaven with angels going up and down on it. "God was in this place, but I, I did not know." Some commentators suggest that this means that Jacob lost his "I" in the midst of the encounter with the Divine.

We call the relationship between God and the individual a covenant. This is just a fancy word for a partnership. We are equal partners, except that God is the senior partner and gets two votes. It is a partnership between God and us that started at the very beginning of recorded time, from the creation of the world.

Whenever we use the traditional form of a blessing, the familiar words *Barukh atah Adonai* . . . , regardless of how we finish the statement, whatever is the focus of our blessing, we have entered into this covenantal relationship with God and affirmed it at the same time. (Amen is the word of affirmation, said by those who hear the blessing, not by those who say it.)

From the very beginning of this series of statements about faith and belief, there emerges the establishment of relationship between the individual and God. Thus, it can be said that the relationship between the individual and God is really at the core of Maimonides' system. It is this covenant, most Jewish theologians argue, that should be the prism through which we view all of Jewish history and practice. If you want to measure the morality of any decision you make, just ask yourself the question, "Does this act reflect my covenantal relationship with God?" Go ahead and try it.

We begin our study for Confirmation the same way. While we might imagine a theologian retreating to a book-filled study, sipping frothy cappuccino, and listening to the inspiring chords of classical music in order to consider the major questions of the life—or even isolating himself or herself on a mountainside or in a forest, near a lake or even on the seaside—the theologian, like most of us, draws conclusions about the world based on his or her interaction and experiences with it. In order to get to the same point as the theologian, try this exercise: Take a walk around your block. As an alternative, you can just stare outside of your bedroom window for a few minutes. The effect should be the same. Make a list of everything you see. Now, take a few moments and think about how they got to the place where you observed them. Then, take an additional step. How did they come into being? Houses and cars are easy to figure out, even the bedroom window itself. We may not know the technical specifics about how they were built or formed, but we do know that they were constructed by people, with the help of lots of different kinds of tools and machines (also made by humans). But what about the trees and the grass and the children playing in the yard? Where did they all come from? Who or what brought that into existence?

The Midrash tells us that there are three partners in the creation of every human being: man, woman, and God.

What do you remember as the first thing you "created"? Was it a project that you brought home from school to show a parent or relative? How is what you "created" related to what God created?

Maimonides calls God the Creator. According to most religious thinkers, this means that God created everything in the world, or, at least, initiated the process of creation which continues today. According to the mystics (the folks who wrote, among other things, the Zohar, the primary book of Jewish mysticism), God contracted Godself (this process is ono-matopoeically called *tzimtzum*) in order to make room for the world. It is a difficult idea to get our minds around, but that's the way the mystics describe it. Then God created the world out of Godself. Thus, they believed that the world is all God. (It's one of the reasons why God is often called *Ha-Makom*, or "The place.")

This first principle of faith includes an explanation of God as Creator. How does Maimonides describe God in this statement? Have you encountered this aspect of God, as Maimonides describes it? And, do you meet this God in the things that you see, the items that you have recorded on your list? What other word might you use to describe your interaction with God?

How does the word "grow" differ from "create"? How does the word "build" differ from "create"?

Often we use the term "create" when we are speaking of new inventions or even art. Is the word used in the same way as it is when we speak of God as the Creator?

To build, we start with materials that already exist. Somehow, the materials had to be created, whether they are natural or synthetic.

There is a story told of a young child who was learning to say thank-you for things. So after eating a meal, she said thank-you to her parents. They responded by saying, "Don't thank us. We only prepared the meal. You must thank the baker who baked the bread." So the child left her home in order to find the baker. When she arrived at the bakery, she was told, "Don't thank me. I only baked the bread. You must thank the miller who ground the grain into flour." So the child left to find the miller. When she arrived at the mill, she was told, "Don't thank me. I only ground the flour. You must thank the farmer who grew the grain." By this time, it was getting late, but she traveled to the edge of town to thank the farmer. When she arrived and said thank you, the farmer said, "Don't thank me. I only planted the seeds. It was God who caused the seeds to grow." Tired, the young child returned home, returned to her parents still sitting at the dinner table, and joined them in reciting birkat ha-mazon (grace after meals) so that they could all thank God together.

In what ways do you thank God for creation?

A Ready Reference

Throughout Jewish literature, there are frequently used phrases that formerly meant something specific, but often no longer have their original meaning due to so much use (and abuse). Often, people repeat them without giving them much thought. We like to call these terms "rabbinisms," because rabbis use them more often than most people do. (Other people just repeat what they hear their rabbis say.) Maimonides uses one such phrase in his first principle. Take a look and see if you can find that word. We modified the principle slightly to make the statement more inclusive (of women as well as men), because we believe that, were Maimonides living today, he would have wanted to include everyone.

Some people use the word "blessed" instead of "praised." The translation "praised" has been chosen because we believe that only God can *bless* us; we are only able to *praise* (and not bless) God. Yet, we *can* become channels through which God's blessing might flow to others and the world in which we live. "A good name is better than fine perfume" (Ecclesiastes 7:1). What do we understand by the word "name"? Certainly, it does not refer to one's family name per se. Rather, it refers to the reputation one has established that is synonymous with one's particular family name. In the same sense, we are praising God's reputation (as good, loving, just, compassionate, etc.), and, by this affirmation, asking God to maintain that reputation by being that way to us as well.

What We Believe

As Maimonides suggests, God is the Author and Guide of all things. What words come to mind when you think of the word "author"? Write them below.

_____

_____

_____

_____

As Maimonides encountered the world, what would have motivated him to choose the word "author" as a description for God? Do you think he wants people to think of the Torah as they read this statement? What else could he have had in mind?

Now do the same thing with the word "guide." What words come to mind when you think of the word "guide"? Write them below.

_____

_____

_____

_____

The term _moreh derekh_ refers to the "teacher of the way." In this way others can guide us on our path through life. (We sometimes refer to these people as "spiritual guides.") Perhaps these people emulate God in some way. Is there anyone in your life who guides you? What have you learned? Do you feel that this person acts on God's behalf?

Why does Maimonides state that God is the Creator "of everything that has been created," and that God "has made, does make, and will make all things"? Why is Maimonides being so specific? Would it not have been enough to say that God is the Creator of the world?

God also has no partner in this process. According to the statement, "God alone" is the Creator of all things. If we are to be partners in creation and to help finish the world that God started, as is held by the rabbis of the Midrash, then how can Maimonides make such a statement?

An Exercise

Open the prayer book to any service. Look for any series of blessings (that's the technical term for statements that begin *Barukh ata Adonai . . .*). Write down how God is described in these blessings. We'll get you started.

Master of the universe

Now go back and circle those items which reflect Maimonides' description of God in this principle of faith. Does the blessing itself agree with what Maimonides is claiming is God's role in the world? How would you describe God's role?

Write a blessing that poetically includes in it what Maimonides is trying to claim about God as the Creator of all.

Extending the Principle of Faith

Rabbi Isaac Luria was a mystic who lived in Safed. He used myths and symbols to explain what he believed about God. Myths are ideas and stories through which a group of people (in our case, the Jewish people) organizes and makes sense of a shared experience. According to Luria's sacred myth, there is a flaw in the world. The flaw developed when God withdrew to make creation possible. According to the way the rabbis understand creation, God created and destroyed many worlds before creating this one. The light that came forth from God during creation was too powerful and too strong for people. The first worlds which God created after the withdrawal were called vessels. This cosmic catastrophe preceded the creation of our own world. Because of this accident, the world we now live in is imperfect. Broken fragments of the vessels have fallen into our world, symbolic of evil. Evil breaks the order of the world, even though God intended the world to be good. But God has given humans the power to combat evil. Sparks of light are symbolic of God's presence, and Luria believed that sparks of God's presence existed in the world imprisoned in the broken fragments of the vessels. It is the task of each and every one of us to free scattered sparks from their shells and reunite them with God. The process of mending the world by reuniting the sparks to return its original state of harmony is called *tikkun,* or repair, and it can be accomplished through the performance of *mitzvot.*

How do you think the performance of *mitzvot* helps to free these sparks and bring the world back to its original harmony?

Reread the first chapter of Genesis, about the very beginning of the creation of the world in the Torah. Determine when humans are created. Some rabbis suggest that the world was left incomplete by God, and that only humans can complete the creation. Make a list of things which we can do to help finish creation. Now, choose one of those things as your confirmation mitzvah project for this year. Call it your *tikkun olam* (repairing the world) project.

Personalizing the Principle of Faith

What does calling God "Creator" mean to you? Make a list of things or events in your life that either confirm or deny your perception of God as Creator. What other words would you use to describe those events?

According to the Bible (take a look at Genesis I again), each human being is made in the image of God. In Hebrew, we call this *b'tzelem Elohim*. Rabbi David Wolpe teaches that this is the reason why we should be proud of ourselves. It is not good grades, or good behavior, or anything else that we accomplish. Instead, it is merely knowing that we are made in the image of God—and therefore, can accomplish these things that should make us feel good about ourselves. Have you ever considered what it means to be created in the image of God? Perhaps it is because we can create—sure, it is on a different scale—just like God. As a matter of fact, the miracle of bringing life into this world (through mother and father) is really an imitation (in the positive sense) of God's unceasing creative activity in the world. What did you do today to act "in the image of God"?

Here's one way the rabbis look at it in the Midrash.

The story is told of Hillel that when he had finished a lesson with his students, he accompanied them part of the way. They said to him, "Teacher, where are you going?" He answered, "To perform a religious duty." They asked, "Which religious duty?" He responded, "To take a bath." They questioned him, "Is that a religious duty?" He answered them, "If somebody is appointed to scrape and clean the statues of the king which are set up in the theaters and circuses, and is paid to do this work, and furthermore, associates with the nobility, how much more so should I, who am created in the divine image and likeness, take care of my body."
(Leviticus Rabbah 34:3)

Do you feel the same way when you bathe or shower?

Textual Encounters

Here are several *midrashim* related to creation. After reading them, try to answer the questions that follow.

Text 1:

Why was the world created with the letter *bet*, the first letter of the Hebrew word bereshit—"in the beginning" (Genesis 1:1)?

Just as the *bet* is closed on three sides and open only in front, so too, you are not permitted to investigate what is above the heavens and what is below the deep, what is before the six days of creation, and what is to happen after the world's existence. You are permitted only that from the time the world was created and thereafter the world we live in.

(Genesis Rabbah 1:10)

Question:

Why were the rabbis concerned that a person not investigate the heavens, the deeps, that which came before creation, and that which will happen after the existence of our world? About what do you think the rabbis were really cautioning people? How does this midrash relate to current scientific inquiry related to space exploration and the exploration of the oceans?

Text 2:

"God created" (Genesis 1:1). It happened that a heretic came to Rabbi Akiva and asked, "This world, who created it?" Rabbi Akiva replied, "The Holy Blessed One." The heretic then said, "Show me clear proof." Rabbi Akiva replied, "Come back to me tomorrow." The next day, when the heretic came, Rabbi Akiva asked him, "What are you wearing?" The heretic replied, "A garment." Rabbi Akiva asked, "Who made it?" The heretic replied: "A weaver." Rabbi Akiva said, "Show me clear proof." The heretic replied, "What could I show you? Don't you know that a weaver made it?"

Rabbi Akiva then asked, "Don't you know that the Holy One made the world?"

After the heretic departed, Rabbi Akiva's disciples asked him, "But what is the clear proof?" Rabbi Akiva replied, "My children, even as a house proclaims its builder, a garment its weaver, or a door its carpenter, so too does the world that the Holy Blessed One created it."

(Talmud, Temura 3)

Question:

What is the Midrash trying to teach? In what way does the very existence of the world proclaim that God created it? Is it possible to prove that God created the world? What is your proof?

Text 3:

If God is the Author and Creator of all, what is the mission of human beings, and how is their mission connected to what God desires of them? The midrash that follows attempts to explain the verse, "You shall walk after Adonai Your God."

Rabbi Hama said, in the name of Rabbi Hanina, "What does it mean, 'You shall walk after Adonai your God'? [Deuteronomy 13:5]. Is it possible for a person to walk and follow God's presence? Does not the Torah teach, 'For Adonai Your God is a consuming fire'? [Deuteronomy 4:24]. But it means that we should walk after the attributes of the Holy Blessed One. Just as God clothes the naked, so you too clothe the naked, as it says, 'Adonai made the man and his wife leather coverings, and clothed them' [Genesis 3:21]. The Holy Blessed One visits the ill, as it says, 'And God visited Abraham in Elonei Mamreh' [Genesis 18:10], so you too shall visit the ill. The Holy Blessed One comforts the bereaved, as it says, 'And it was after Abraham died and that God blessed his son Isaac,' so you too shall comfort the bereaved. The Holy Blessed One buries the dead, as it says, 'And God buried Moses in the valley' [Deuteronomy 34:6], so you too shall bury the dead."

Questions:

What is this midrash trying to teach? In what ways does God, Author, and Creator of the world, need human beings for assistance? What are some of the things that God needs human beings to create?

Text 4:

Here is a text from the Talmud. Try to find the prayer in the morning service that describes God as Creator in the same way.

"A human being can cut a form on a wall but cannot make breath, a soul, organs, or intestines in it. But the Holy Blessed One fashions forms within forms and gives them breath, a soul, and all the organs needed for life."

(Talmud, Megillah 14a)

How Judaism Differs

Judaism and Christianity agree on the view of God as Creator. Interview a Christian friend. Ask him or her what he/she is taught about God and creation in his/her church. Compare it to your own views.

Christianity also believes that the material world is tainted by imperfection. Compare this idea with the idea of the broken vessels of Isaac Luria.

From Faith to Deeds

According to our understanding of the Torah, when Adam and Eve lived in the Garden of Eden they were immortal. They became mortal only after eating of the tree of knowledge of good and evil, for which they were expelled from the Garden. The story had to happen this way if it is to reflect human reality. Like the first man and woman, we are not immortal. However, we can imitate the immortality of God through the process of procreation, or the bearing of children.

Because we are so preoccupied as teenagers with moral decision making regarding sex and the fear of pregnancy and sexually transmitted diseases (STDs), we forget about the important role it can have in our lives—under the right circumstances and in the right contexts. In a certain way, we imitate God through the bearing of children. God created us in such a way that we could continue the creation that was started at the beginning of the world. Some would argue, therefore, that the only reason for sex is for the bearing of children. Others might say that if God had wanted it for that purpose alone, why did God make it so much fun? At any rate, sex is serious business. What do you think?

Of course, there are other ways of being remembered long after we are gone, particularly by the things we teach and the ways we influence others. However, procreation is the closest we can get to immortality.

How does this idea fit into your moral reasoning regarding sex?

According to the rabbis, there are thirty-nine kinds of labor that we are prohibited from doing on Shabbat. (If you want to see the original discussion, take a look at the Talmud, Shabbat 106a.) The rabbis compiled this list by looking at the specific tasks done to complete the building of the ancient Tabernacle. Here is the list:

Baking; bleaching; building; carrying in a public place; combing raw material; cutting to shape; demolishing; dyeing; erasing; extinguishing a fire; grinding; inserting thread in a loom; kindling a fire; kneading; marking out; plowing; reaping; removing the finished article; scraping; selecting; separating into threads; sewing; sheaf making; sheepshearing; sifting; skinning or flaying; slaughtering; sowing; spinning; tanning; tearing; the final hammer blow; threshing; trapping; tying a knot; untying a knot; weaving; winnowing; and writing.

The various Jewish religious movements have different perspectives on these labors and their particular understandings of what is prohibited on Shabbat. How do you think that these labors are related to God as Creator?

While the Conservative movement often speaks of specific requirements that make Shabbat special, the Reform movement uses the term the "spirit of Shabbat." In other words, what activities may be allowed or prohibited for the sake of preserving the spirit of Shabbat. Make your own list here. Be prepared to defend your position.

As part of your personal observance, what might you not do on Shabbat?

Godtalk

It may sound contradictory, but Shabbat is a special time that is also timeless. We set aside our watches on this day so that we are not preoccupied with schedules. Even the normal twenty-four-hour day changes on Shabbat (which is extended to twenty-five hours). It sounds strange, but we have the opportunity to experience paradise, a foretaste of the world-to-come during Shabbat.

How can that happen? What can we do to make it happen?

However we choose to observe Shabbat, it is also the time when, by ceasing from creation, we acknowledge that we are not immortal. For one day a week, we simply let the world alone. God rested on the Sabbath, and God gave us the Sabbath on which we too can rest.

What Can We Believe?

The struggle for most moderns with regard to this first principle of faith can be divided into two areas. First, its apparent disagreement with science over how the world came into being (e.g., the "Big Bang" theory). The second is its apparent conflict with what we have learned as the process of evolution in science. Begin by writing down what science has to say about the creation of the world.

_____

_____

_____

_____

Now, compare it to how the Torah depicts the world's creation. Make a list of the differences. Without using the argument that the Torah is an ancient document and hence, did not know what scientists today know, consider why the Torah emphasizes certain things. For example, the Big Bang theory argues that the creation of the world was originated with an accidental explosion. The Torah suggests that the creation of the world was orderly and calculated, thought through by God.

Now, write down what you have learned about the evolution of the human species according to modern science.

_____

_____

_____

_____

How does what you wrote conflict with what you have learned in religious school about the creation of the world?

The Spectrum of Jewish Belief: Reform, Conservative, and All the Rest

The Reform movement believes that what we have discovered about the world and about human beings is part of the revelation of God. Therefore, Torah and science are complementary. However, since the Torah is not attempting to scientifically explain the origin of the world or of humankind, we can't expect it to be scientifically accurate. Instead, it is a spiritual document that wants to teach us other truths about the world and how we came into being.

Many Conservative thinkers accept the idea that God revealed the Torah to Israel. But there are some who believe that the revealing of Torah, or revelation, happened only once in history, while others consider revelation to be an ongoing process in which each generation of Jews uncovers more and more of God's word. The reason that Conservative Jews cannot accept the Orthodox position, that the Torah is the complete and final word of God, is because, then, change and growth would be impossible.

Nor can they agree with many in the Reform movement who hold that only the ethical rules are God-given, since it may very well be that God is concerned with the observance of ritual laws as well as ethical ones. Most Conservative Jews believe that revelation is a dialogue between God and humanity. Thus, the Bible and Jewish law is the response of humanity to God's call, and the mitzva is the human interpretation and application of Divine principles.

Following Mordecai Kaplan, Reconstructionists generally believe that the Bible is not the record of God's word to people but the search of people for God. Whenever one discovers a religious truth or great moral idea, it is for us a revelation of God's will. For Reconstructionists, *mitzvot* are folkways or customs, the purpose of which is to bring people closer to God and to help them lead more meaningful lives. Thus, for Reconstructionist Jews, observing a ritual such as Shabbat is not done because God commanded the Israelites to do so and it is therefore a mitzvah, but rather, because observing the Sabbath teaches us the importance of rest, and it helps us to survive as one people by uniting us.

Orthodox Judaism believes the Torah was revealed by God. Therefore, it is our obligation to try to figure out how to reconcile science with the Torah. While centrist, or middle-of-the-road, Orthodoxy believes that science is relevant, right-wing Orthodox Jews believe that there is no basis for comparison at all between secular knowledge and religious truths.

PRINCIPLE TWO

The Unity of God

I believe with perfect faith that the Creator, praised be Your name, is a Unity, and that there is no unity in any manner like You, and that You alone are our God, who was, is, and will be.

Getting Started: Some Background

Moses Maimonides championed an approach to Jewish theology called the theory of negative attributes. He argued that whenever we speak about God—and use adjectives, however numerous and extensive, to describe the Deity—we actually diminish our praise of God. Since we can never fully describe God, we are better off not trying to describe God at all. Thus, Maimonides is very careful about what words he uses when he writes about God.

Have you ever been in a situation in which a teacher thanks everyone who helped on a particular project, naming all those individuals who come to mind? If the teacher leaves out a person—and this often happens to all of us—it diminishes the praise given to everyone. So goes the argument that the teacher is better off not naming individuals. It is the same thing when we begin to "name" the various attributes of God.

Here is a partial list of names of God that are used in the prayer book and Bible. Look at the list, and take from it those names which describe the way in which you believe in God.

1. Lord (*Adonai*)
2. King, Ruler (*Melech*)

3. Mighty One of Jacob (*Elohay Ya'akov*)

4. Eternal God (*Adon Olam*)

5. I am that I am (*Ehyeh Asher Ehyeh*)

6. Lord of Hosts (*Adonai Tzeva'ot*)

7. My Shepherd (*Ro'ee*)

8. Rock of Israel (*Tzur Yisrael*)

9. Shield of Abraham (*Magen Avraham*), Helper of Sarah (*Pokayd Sara*)

10. King of Kings, Sovereign of Sovereigns (*Melech Malchay ha-Melachim*)

11. Peace (*Shalom*)

12. The Holy One (*Ha-Kadosh*), The Holy Blessed One, The Holy One of Blessing (*Ha-kadosh Barukh Hu*)

13. The Faithful One (*Ha-Ne'eman*)

14. Our Father [Our Parent] in Heaven (*Avinu she-Bashamayim*)

15. Our Healer (*Rofaynu*)

16. The Compassionate One (*Ha-Rachaman*)

17. God, Man [Person] of War (*Adonai Ish Milchama*)

18. The Generous One (*Ha-Gomel Chesed*)

19. The Place (*Ha-Makom*)

20. The Awesome One (*Ha-Nora*)

21. Shekhinah (*God's Presence*)

22. Source of Life (*Mekor Chayim*)

Are there other words which you would use to describe God? Have you ever used them in addressing God to enhance your prayer experience?

Try to isolate one incident in which you felt or encountered God's presence. Using as many adjectives as you think are appropriate, try to describe your experience of God in that moment. After you have made the list, consider what made you stop writing. Did you run out of words?

"Perfect Faith"

While we discussed the idea of "perfect faith" in the previous chapter, we must consider it once again in relationship to Maimonides' second principle of faith. (We will look at this idea again in subsequent chapters.) Some religious traditions encourage an unwavering faith in God. They argue that certain, or "perfect" faith provides us with tranquility, serenity in addition to surety. Alternatively, Jewish scholars suggest that individuals should constantly struggle with their beliefs—and with God. Like the biblical patriarch Jacob, Jews should all be "wrestlers with God." This constant dialogue is what gives us certainty—or "perfect faith"—for in the context of dialogue, a relationship develops between God and us. This evolving relationship is what we like to call the covenant. This dialogue is not always constant or steady. We may not always be able to speak clearly or hear God communicate to us distinctly. At times, the relationship is strained, thus making communication more difficult. Nevertheless, the relationship itself is always reliable. When we use the familiar formula for blessing (*Barukh ata Adonai . . .*), and we are instructed to "bless" (or thank) God for the good and for the evil, however difficult it is to do so, it works the same way. By uttering words of blessing we foster our relationship with God. The rabbis suggest that we should try to say at least one hundred blessings every day. Try it yourself. Begin with those blessings with which you may already be familiar—and then add all the blessings for those things for which you are supposed to say a blessing. (Take a look at our *How to Handbooks for Jewish Living* for help.) This approach will surely maintain the dialogue. How many blessings did you offer to God today? Why not keep a journal so that you can look back at your relationship with God and see how it grows and evolves each day.

A Ready Reference
The Theory of Negative Attributes

The theory of negative attributes in Judaism was formulated by the renowned medieval philosopher Moses Maimonides. He taught that when we use human language to talk about God, we are only being poetic, metaphorical. God is so totally other that one cannot adequately describe God with words borrowed from descriptions of human beings. Yet, we must talk about God and strive to understand God. Thus, Maimonides held that we can speak accurately (as opposed to poetically) about God only when we speak negatively, when we deny inaccurate statements about God. This is because God is a simple being, and any positive attributes, such as "powerful" or "merciful," would imply that these qualities are, as it were, "added" to the simple nature of God, making God a composite being. The only attributes that can possibly be applied to God are those which derive from God's effects on us. These must be understood properly. For example, "God is merciful" simply means that God acts mercifully. Thus according to Maimonides, the only real attributes of God, especially those that express God's essence, are the negative ones. For example, when we state that "God is one," it does not mean that "oneness" is added to God. Rather, it means that "God is not many" and that "God has no equal." Similarly, to say that "God hears our prayers" does not explain anything about God. Rather, it rejects the idea that praying is a waste of time.

Blessed Be Your Name

Following Jewish tradition, Maimonides uses the phrase "Blessed be Your Name" whenever he writes about God. The practice is similar to the approach taken in the synagogue worship service. Whenever the *shaliach tzibur* (prayer service leader) mentions God's name in the context of the formula for blessing, *Barukh ata Adonai* ("Praised is God"), worshipers immediately respond *Barukh hu u'varukh sh'mo* ("Praised are You and Praised is Your Name"). While some people respond to it in a rather knee-jerk way, without really thinking about what they are saying or doing, it is really an opportunity to claim the attention of worshipers when God's name is spoken. It is also a way to nurture a dialogue between the *shatz* (acronym for *shaliach tzibur*) and the congregation, and to refocus our concentration on our prayer.

What's in a Name?

Why do thinkers like Maimonides spend so much time focusing on the name of God? This stems from an ancient belief that when you speak someone's name you have entered into an intimate relationship with that individual. Moreover, we are somehow able to see through to an individual's essence when speaking the person's name. That is why only the High Priest, and only on Yom Kippur, spoke God's "personal" four-letter name (usually written as YHVH). One of our teachers, Rabbi Chanan Brichto, of blessed memory, liked to think of the four-letter name of God as "yoo-hoo" (the way you may call out to a friend at a distance) in order to emphasize its intimate, familiar, personal quality. Because of the awesome power associated with God's name, it was only spoken in the innermost chamber of the ancient Temple in Jerusalem (what was called the Holy of Holies). Various customs have developed throughout Jewish history to prevent us from speaking God's name casually, without thinking. What are some of these customs?

But it is more than just God's name. It is God's reputation to which Maimonides is really referring. According to Jewish tradition, we are known by three names. The first is the one given to us by our parents. The second is the one by which we are known to others. The third is the one which we earn through our actions.

What about your name? What do people call you? How did you get that name?

When do you use the term "name" to refer to someone's reputation?

The Creator

In the first principle Maimonides stated that God is the Creator. God created the world and all that is in it, including all of us. Now, Maimonides is prepared to build his second principle of faith on this indispensable foundation of belief which he taught in principle no. I. Are you prepared to do the same?

What do you consider to be God's most unusual creation?

What aspect of creation do you understand least?

What do you think should not have been created?

How do you feel about things that God created that are now extinct?

What can we do to make sure that others of God's creations are not forced into extinction?

God's Unity

While we may experience God through many divine attributes, they are expressions of the same God. Take a look at a precious stone. If you do not have one of your own, perhaps on a ring, maybe a parent or friend has one that you can look at. A precious gem might look different depending on how the light is reflected on its various facets; yet, it is the same gemstone.

God—Who Was, Is, and Always Will Be

We measure our lives and human history over time. However, according to Maimonides, God is beyond all time. God transcends time. This is a difficult notion to consider, particularly when thinking about the creation of the world and of humankind. One tradition suggests that we cannot even speculate on time before the creation of the world. It's one of the reasons given for starting the Torah with the Hebrew letter *bet* for *bereishit* ("in the beginning"). Its very shape suggests that what came before is closed off from us. (With the help of your rabbi, open the Torah scroll, and see how this *bet* is shaped.)

Likewise, when we think about the future, the time of the messiah, it too is a time that is beyond the measurement of time as we know it. (We will discuss messianism in chapter 12.)

How do you reconcile the Genesis story with what you have learned about evolution?

What We Believe

The ideas in this principle are rather abstract. It is hard to conceive of all this as beyond everything in our everyday experience. What do we believe about God? Try rewriting this principle in your own words based on what you have learned so far in your Confirmation class and what you have experienced in your life. Consider why it is so important to be able to articulate your beliefs in writing.

An Exercise

Just being alive raises deep and fundamental questions and doubts. This is the same to decide whether you consider yourself religious or not. Here are some questions that will help you to test your faith about God? Be as honest as possible in answering the questions:

1. What are some of your doubts about God?
2. Have you ever felt that God was talking to you?
3. When have you felt closest to God?
4. Has God ever answered any of your prayers?
5. Is there anything that makes you angry about God?
6. If you were God, what would you do differently?

Extending the Principle of Faith

That there are many questions about God which are not fully answered does not mean that our beliefs on these issues do not matter. On the contrary, they can change the world. For what an individual believes about God will both shape and reflect his or her deepest commitments in life. For example, a people that believes in a God who "adopts orphans and widows" and directs us to do likewise will construct a society vastly different from that of a community which glorifies only the autonomy of human beings.

This chapter has dealt with Maimonides' second principle of faith, concentrating on the unity of God. Some have said that a belief in the unity of God will help to create and reinforce a belief in the unity of humanity and a commitment to standards of justice and ethics. Do you agree with this statement? What other actions might people who believe strongly in God's unity take with regard to their commitments to humanity? What behavioral patterns might the Christian concept of a Trinity—the united Godhead of three divine persons: the Father, the Son (Jesus), and the Holy Spirit—lead to for people of Christian faith? How different is their concept of the Trinity from that of God's unity?

Personalizing the Principle of Faith

Many people imagine that philosophers and theologians spend their days just thinking about these ideas. Sometimes we imagine theologians isolating themselves in a study, filled from wall to ceiling with books, then sitting down at a desk (and, of course, a computer) to figure out specific ideas about God. This is usually not the way it goes. Instead, ideas about God—even for philosophers and theologians—grow out of everyday interaction with the world. This section of the chapter helps you to grapple with the principle, just like a philosopher or theologian, and make it your own.

In order to do so, find a way in which you can relate to the idea in your own everyday life.

What do you do everyday that causes you to think about God in the way described by this principle?

Textual Encounters

Here are several passages taken from biblical and rabbinic texts. Each deals with the relationship of a people to God. After reading each passage, questions will follow which will give you a chance to organize your own theology.

Text I: Should Humankind Have Been Created?

In this rabbinic encounter, God and God's angels are talking to each other.

> Rabbi Simon said, "When the Holy One was about to create Adam, the ministering angels formed themselves into groups, some of them saying, 'Let Adam be created,' while others urged, 'Let Adam not be created.' Thus it is written, 'Love and truth fought together, righteousness and peace combated each other' [Psalm 85:11]. Love then said, 'Let Adam be created, because he will perform acts of love.' Truth said, 'Let Adam not be created, because all of Adam will be falsehood.' Righteousness said, 'Let Adam be created, because Adam will do righteous deeds.' Peace said, 'Let Adam not be created, because Adam will be all strife.' What did the Holy One do? God took truth and cast it to the ground, as is said, 'You did cast down truth to the ground' [Daniel 8:12]. The ministering angels dared to say to the Holy One, 'Master of the Universe, why do You humiliate Your seal (i.e., truth)? Let truth arise from the earth.' Thus it is written, 'Let truth spring up from the earth' [Psalm 85:12].
> (Genesis Rabbah 8:5)

Questions:

Why did Truth have to be cast to the ground (i.e., thrown out) before humans could be created? Why do you think that God chose the advice of Mercy over that of Truth? What would occur now if humans were judged primarily by the standard of truth? What question do you think this midrash is attempting to answer, and what does it tell us about God?

Text 2: The Destruction of the World

The following biblical text describes God's change of heart after the creation of the world.

> The earth became corrupt before God and was filled with lawlessness. When God saw how corrupt the earth was, for all flesh had corrupted its ways on earth, God said to Noah, "I have decided to put an end to all flesh, for the earth is filled with lawlessness because of them. I am about to destroy them with the earth. Make yourself an ark of gopher wood. . . ."
> (Genesis 6:11–14)

Questions:

What do you believe was the monstrous evil that brought on God's judgment? Why do you think that God deemed it necessary to destroy the entire world which God had created? One of the traditional Jewish beliefs about God is the that God is all-knowing and all-powerful? If this is so, why did God not create a world that would be good, so that there should not have been the need for its destruction? What does this tell us about God?

Text 3: Abraham's Argument with God

The following biblical narrative describes Abraham's dramatic confrontation with God. Here are several excerpts from the narrative:

> God said, "The outrage of Sodom and Gomorrah is so great, and their sin is so grave! I will go down to see whether they have acted altogether according to the outcry that has come to Me. If not, I will take note." The men went on from there to Sodom, while Abraham remained standing before God. Abraham then went forward and said, "Will You sweep away the innocent along with the guilty? What if there should be fifty innocent within the

city, will You then wipe out the place and not forgive it for the sake of the innocent fifty who are in it? Far be it from You to do such a thing, to bring death upon the innocent as well as the guilty, so that innocent and guilty fare alike. Far be it from you! Shall not the Judge of all the earth deal justly? And God answered, "If I find within the city of Sodom fifty innocent ones, I will forgive the whole place for their sake."

(Don't forget that by the end of the narrative, Abraham cannot find even ten innocent people, and the dialogue between Abraham and God ceases. All the people in Sodom and Gemorrah are destroyed.)

Questions:

Do you think that Abraham is doubting God's justice in this story? Is it proper for any human being to doubt any action of God? Why do you think God was willing to save the cities of Sodom and Gemorrah if Abraham were able to find fifty innocent people? Why do you think the Bible ends its story with the inability of Abraham to find ten innocent people?

Text 4: Four Who Entered Paradise

Four scholars entered paradise (they engaged in esoteric philosophy and mysticism): Ben Azzai, Ben Zoma, Acher, and Rabbi Akiva. Ben Azzai cast a look and died. Ben Zoma looked and became demented. Elisha ben Abuyah (called Acher, the other) looked into the divine secrets and destroyed the plans. (That means he became a heretic.) Only Rabbi Akiva departed unharmed.

(Talmud, Hagigah 14b)

Questions:

What is the lesson this rabbinic statement is attempting to teach us. Do you think that there are any forbidden regions of the divine mystery? If so, what are they?

How Judaism Differs

There are many different Christian denominations. They differ on a variety of religious principles. However, they all accept the idea of the Trinity: that God has three distinct aspects, and is experienced as Father, Son, and Holy Spirit. Judaism, on the other hand, experiences God as an indivisible unity. It is this distinction that was among the reasons that Maimonides wrote this principle. Perhaps a Christian friend may be willing to discuss his or her understanding of the Trinity with you.

From Faith to Deeds

At Sinai, our people responded to the giving of Torah with these words: "We will do and we will listen." It seems like an odd construction of words. We would expect that "listening" would come before "doing." Some people suggest that doing leads to understanding. Others suggest that the phrase means that the Israelites were telling God that God would know that they had listened by seeing what they had done. In any case, Judaism teaches that belief must be accompanied by action. What is it about this principle that propels us to action?

Godtalk

Following are some sentence completions to help you bring your beliefs concerning God into focus:

1. I most need God when

2. I feel closest to God when

3. I am most likely to pray to God when

4. I like to thank God when

5. I have struggled with God when

6. I sometimes doubt God when

7. I believe in God when

8. I have seen God perform miracles when

9. I wonder about God when

10. People most need God when

11. God most needs people when

12. I most feel like a chosen person of God when`

13. To believe in God means

14. Not to believe in God means

15. My belief about God is

16. For me, God is

17. God's most important attribute is

18. I feel God's love when

19. I most feel God's anger when

20. I am most likely to call upon God when

What Can We Believe?

Some of us are still struggling with our belief in God and our understanding of the divine. It is normal for everyone to wrestle with God. Our ancestors did so, as well. Consider Jacob wrestling with the angel in the middle of the night. Most rabbis interpret this as Jacob grappling with God. That's why they call him a "Godwrestler." Moreover, just as we develop over time in various ways, our faith is also developing and growing. So you can expect your beliefs to change over time. They will grow and evolve just as you do.

The Spectrum of Jewish Belief: Reform, Conservative, and All the Rest

This is perhaps the one principle that draws little disagreement among the various major Jewish movements. All these movements agree that this unity principle unites them. Historian Ellis Rivkin argues that this is the common thread in Judaism, and that it can easily be discerned throughout Jewish history, regardless of community or time.

PRINCIPLE THREE

The Shape and Form of God

I believe with perfect faith that the Creator, praised be Your name, is not a body, and that You are free from all the accidents of matter, and that You have not any form whatsoever.

Getting Started: Some Background

This is a tough one. But the truth is that all of Maimonides' principles are tough. That's why they call it philosophy. This one just seems more difficult, because it forces us to think about something that is by definition beyond our ability to comprehend. How do we express ourselves about God when we are limited by words and images that primarily come to us through our experience as human beings? Because God is God, God is beyond our ability to describe in words or images, no matter how hard we try. This is one of the reasons why, when we experience the Divine in our lives, it is nearly impossible to explain what we have experienced to another person.

Some people say that faith is kind of like love. How do you tell others what love feels like? Or what love is? You might be able to tell people how to express their love to another, but try describing it. Instead, we often say, "You'll know what love is when you're in it." And that is the best you can do. But philosophers and theologians are not satisfied with this kind of explanation. So they work harder to try to get us to understand.

Even though we believe that God has no form or body, we use our experience as human beings to talk about God. These are the words and ideas that make up our vocabulary, what we like to call our "universe of discourse." For example, when we talk about our deliverance from Egypt, we say that God brought us out of Egypt "with a strong hand and an outstretched arm" (Deuteronomy 4:34). What do you suggest as an alternative way of expressing the same thing? According to Jewish tradition, *Bekhol dor vador chayav adam lirot et atzmo k'ilu hu yatza miMitzrayim,*. "All of us are required to look at ourselves as if we had been personally delivered from Egypt." So, describe how it felt to be delivered "by the hand of God."

Make a list of other phrases that you know from the Bible or from the siddur which express things about God that are borrowed from the human experience. Next to each description, try to explain what the writer is really trying to suggest.

_____

_____

_____

_____   _____

_____   _____

How often do you describe God using words that reflect human action or emotion—even in terms of everyday speech? Make a list below. Then, next to the list, offer an alternative way of saying the same thing.

_____

_____

_____

_____

_____

A Ready Reference

Anthropomorphism: the assigning of human activity or form to God. For example, we may speak of "staying God's hand" when we mean trying to prevent God from doing something. Or we may say "the mind of God" when we talk about God thinking (this too is a human kind of activity).

Anthropopathism: the assigning of human emotion to God. For example, when God was sad and wept after the destruction of the Egyptians (who were also God's creation) in the Red Sea.

Keviyakhol (literally, as if you were able [to do so]). This word is used after describing God with words that are often used to describe human activity or emotion. Try using it in a sentence after you have described God in such a way.

What We Believe

Jews believe a lot of things about God, particularly about what God is and what God is not. For example, some theologians believe that God is totally other, that is, completely separate from human beings and the world. We use the word *transcendent* to describe God this way. (Because of this distance, this also means that we cannot have a direct, intimate relationship with God. Likewise, God's presence is felt in an impersonal way.) Others believe that God is in the world and the world is in God. We call this form of belief *pantheism*. What other ways are there to describe God? (This one may take some library research.)

As a result of this struggle of how to describe, throughout history Jewish artists have generally avoided representing God graphically. This may also be a result of the way some people interpret the commandment "Don't make for yourselves an idol that is in the form of anything that is above or below." (Check this out for yourself: Exodus 20:4.) Take a look around your synagogue. Make a list of any place where you see God represented or personified. Next to this, write down how God is described or represented. Remember to include things like the *ner tamid* (eternal light) which also reminds us of God's presence through perpetual illumination.

In this principle, Maimonides tells us that God is free from "accidents of matter." What actually is an accident of matter? Does it refer to all things material or only to those that are not formed in an orderly fashion? Perhaps by using the term "accident," Maimonides is suggesting that when something is corporeal, that is, made of matter, it is "corrupt" (imperfect). Therefore, God (even though God is the Creator of all things) is removed from it.

Some ancient philosophers argued that everything material has an immaterial form. This form is like a template which, when combined with raw matter, shapes a particular object. Thus, there is a form for all things, including ideas. Maimonides teaches that God has no form whatsoever, because God is unlike everything that exists in the world.

An Exercise

Find a relaxing place for this exercise. The idea here is to reduce outside stimuli and distraction as much as possible. If you are inside, turn off the lights. If outside light is peering in through the windows, then close the drapes. If you are outside, find a place that is quiet with few people to disturb you. Try to relax your entire body, a little at a time. First, relax your toes, then, your legs and the lower part of your body. Keep going until you are fully relaxed. Then, consciously remove any thought that comes to mind. Imagine that you are reaching inside of yourself and removing it. One by one, empty your mind entirely of all its images or thoughts. Then, try to conceive of God without form or body, making sure that you don't borrow anything from any thoughts that might still be lingering in your mind. Afterwards, attempt to describe your thoughts to someone else.

Extending the Principle of Faith

Synagogues are filled with religious art, but it is not always hung on the walls as you might expect it to be. Often the architecture of the building itself reflects the religious beliefs of a particular community. With your classmates, take a walking tour of your synagogue. Go from room to room, from space to space, recording all of its art. Take an inventory of the entire synagogue. (If your synagogue is large, divide the project with your classmates.) Remember that you can find Jewish art depicted in ritual objects as well. Use the form on the next page for your work. Feel free to photocopy it if necessary. As you go through each room, pay attention to how God is depicted, and fill out the form for each category listed. If what you have seems to be in agreement with Maimonides' principle no. 3, place a check mark next to the item.

Room/Space

Object

General scene

How God is described/depicted

Let's take a look at how the language of prayer helps us to understand this principle. Choose a prayer from Shabbat (either the evening or morning service). Read it through slowly. Write down all of the ways in which the prayer describes God. Then, determine how the description leads us into thinking of God in "bodily" terms. For example, if God is described as the *Melekh Ha-Olam*, or King of the Universe, then you might imagine God as a male king sitting on a throne with a crown on his head. How would your mental construct change if we translated *Melekh Ha-Olam* as Sovereign Ruler of the Universe? What description could we use that would describe God as powerful without forcing us to draw conclusions about what God looks like? How about Guide of Humanity? Once you have come up with some alternative suggestions, try reciting the prayer with them. (Some people are uncomfortable with the idea of changing the traditional language of prayer, so they will translate it differently. Others will not touch the language at all, and teach themselves to think of alternative images when reciting the traditional words.)

Now, try a similar approach with this week's Torah or Haftarah portion. Choose a selection of text, and determine how it tries to communicate the image of God to the reader.

Personalizing the Principle of Faith

Some people take issue with the exclusivity of traditional prayer language. They feel that if God is depicted in a certain way, particularly as a male, that image gets in the way of developing a more pure conception of the divine (and of a relationship with God). So they go about changing the pronouns, first in English (and in Hebrew for those who are bold enough). This is an important first step. Try it yourself below. Stick with the English. We will work on the Hebrew at a different time! Take a blessing or a few lines of a prayer which is familiar to you, and try to rewrite the English (without disturbing the content or context of the prayer) so that the language is gender neutral, as we have done in this book.

From: To:

_____

_____

_____

_____

Often we change the pronoun from He to You. This changes the "royal" third person, like His honor or His majesty to the second person. This form is used when we want to speak directly to a person but refer to that person in the third person anyway as a sign of respect and distance. In doing so, we have done more than just change the pronoun. We have moved from the relationship between king and subject to the more intimate relationship of covenantal partners. After all, prayer is about developing and maintaining the relationship between individuals and God. (We've done it ourselves in the way in which we have translated Maimonides' Thirteen Principles of Faith.)

Now, here's a slightly more difficult challenge. Go through the same blessing or prayer, and change the metaphor from one that is laden with male characteristics to one that is gender neutral. Often God is described using images that, in the societies in which the liturgy was composed, are decidedly male. We'll get you started.

From: To:

Melekh Ha-Olam, King of the Universe   Guide of the Universe

_____

_____

_____

_____

How does the use of these prayer ideas change how you relate to the prayers and ultimately, to God? Invite your friends to comment on the same question. Do boys feel differently about them than girls? What about men and women? Is this a difference between differing ages or generations?

Each of us conceives of God in his or her own way. In fact, almost everything that has been written about God is a human imaging of God. This is undoubtedly why God has been denominated in the Bible and the prayer book with so many different names. Here are some different appellations that have been used for God. Which names have you heard? Which strike a responsive chord in you? Which do you find comfortable? Which cause you to think?

1. Adonai
2. Elohim
3. Rock of Ages (*Ma'oz Tzur*)
4. God of our [ancestors] Abraham, Isaac, Jacob (*Elohei Avraham, Yitzchak, ve-Ya'akov*) Sarah, Rebecca, Rachel, Leah (*Elohei Sarah, Elohei Rivka, Elohei Rachel velohei Leah*)
5. I am what I am (*Ehyeh asher Ehyeh*)
6. Great and Awesome One (*El Ram ve-Norah*)
7. Reviver of the Dead (*Mechayei Ha-Maytim*)
8. The Merciful One (*Ha-Rachaman*)
9. The Eternal One (*Adon Olam*)
10. Healer (*Rofe*)
11. Shepherd (*Ro'eh*)
12. God of Hosts (*Adonai Tzevaot*)
13. Our Parent in Heaven (*Avinu she-bashamayim*)
14. Sovereign of Sovereigns (*Melekh Malkhei Ha-Melekhim*)
15. Peace (*Shalom*)

Textual Encounters

Usually we think of the Shema as only two short lines of text. While most Reform congregations speak both of them aloud while standing, other synagogues say only the first line aloud and utter the second line to themselves in an undertone. In reality, the Shema is much longer. Jewish tradition considers the Shema (and its blessings) as an entire unit of text. But let's just look at the two basic lines:

Shema Yisrael Adonai Elohenu Adonai Echad.
Barukh Shem kavod malkhuto leolam vaed.

Usually, we translate the lines something like this:
Hear! O Israel, Adonai is our God, Adonai is One.
Praised be God's Name forever and ever.

Now, let's try translating it with a little help:
Pay attention, O people Israel.
Adonai (that's YHVH, the personal God of Israel) is (the same God as) Elohenu (the awesome power of the universe with whom there is no way of communicating or reaching), and Adonai is One (both experiences of God are one and the same).

This is the liturgy's way of bringing together two disparate ideas about God. (1) God is personal and easily accessible. We are so intimate with the Divine that we are on a "first name" basis, *keviyakhol* (i.e., YHVH). (2) God is distant, and is beyond our ability to communicate. God is busy with the forces of law and of nature that guide our lives, having set them in motion at Creation (i.e., Elohim).

In order to fully benefit from the lesson of this text, we recommend that you try chanting the two lines of the Shema softly. Use your entire breath to say each word. Then, take a breath before saying the next word. In this way, the Shema becomes a *kavanna*, or a Jewish mantra, for us. It also gives meaning to the very last line of the Book of Psalms: *Kol ha-neshama tehalel Yah*/Let every breath praise God.

In Exodus 33:18, Moses addresses God: "Show me Your Presence." God's answer appears five verses later, "I will take My hand away and you will see My back, but My face must not be seen" (Exodus 33:23).

What does Moses mean when he asks God to reveal the Divine Presence? Are there times when you have felt God's Presence? How did you feel?

What do you think the text means when it quotes God's response to Moses? What exactly is God's back and God's face?

In Genesis, God said, "Let us make the human in our image, after our likeness. Then God created the human in the divine image" (Genesis 1:26–27).

What does the image of God refer to in these verses? According to Maimonides' *Guide for the Perplexed*, the image does not refer to the physical form of the human or of God. Rather, it is a metaphor that refers to endowing humans with rational faculties.

Take out your family's photo album. What does it mean when someone looks at it and says, "You are a picture of your mother or your father. How does this relate to human beings made in God's image? What non-physical things affect our lives? How do they resemble God?

Here's a story from the Talmud (Chullin 59b) that makes the point a little differently. What do you think?

> Rabbi Joshua ben Hananiah once traveled to Rome to speak with Emperor Hadrian on behalf of the Jewish people. The emperor had enacted some laws that made life very difficult for them, especially a law requiring that they worship Roman gods.
>
> Over the years, whenever they met, Hadrian had always tried to stump Rabbi Joshua with difficult questions about life and religion, but Rabbi Joshua had always been able to answer them. This time, however, the emperor had a very tough question for the rabbi. "Our gods," said Hadrian, "have faces, but yours does not. I want to know what your God looks like."

Rabbi Joshua replied, "It says in the Bible that no human being can see God and live."

"Nonsense. Who would believe in a God that you cannot see?"

Rabbi Joshua realized that he made a mistake. Hadrian might now decide to make the laws even stricter and totally deny the Jews their religious freedom.

Finally, Rabbi Joshua said, "Come outside with me and I will show you my answer."

Emperor Hadrian followed Rabbi Joshua into the hot, bright palace courtyard. Rabbi Joshua faced the emperor.

"You must look up straight at the sun to discover our God," he said.

"But I can't do that," the emperor replied. "You know that no one can look directly at the sun."

"If you can't look directly at the sun's face, how do you expect to be able to look at God's face?" asked Rabbi Joshua. "The sun is merely a servant of God, and its brilliance is nothing compared to God's brilliance and presence."

Emperor Hadrian had no answer to give to Rabbi Joshua, and he dismissed him. The rabbi returned home and continued to pray to his God that no one could see.

If God has no body or form, what do you make out of this talmudic text? "Rabbi Nachman bar Yitzchak adds, 'What is written on the tefillin of the Master of the Universe?' He replied, 'And who is like Your people Israel, a unique nation on earth?'" (Babylonian Talmud, Berakhot 6a).

How Judaism differs

Christianity takes the idea of corrupted matter much further and extends it to human beings as well, who are corrupt as a result of the sin (and subsequent sexual union) of Adam and Eve. This means that Christianity maintains that sexuality is somewhat tainted. It is a necessity to bring children into the world, but the act itself is sullied. How does this idea differ from the Jewish view of sexuality?

In addition, according to Christianity, God appeared in human form as Jesus. While Judaism acknowledges the presence of God in our midst (and calls it the *Shekhina*), this presence is not in human form.

From Faith to Deeds

The biggest challenge of Confirmation, and adult life in general, is acting upon your beliefs. It is about no longer taking the cue for your religious and moral decisions from your peers. Rather, you begin to listen to your inner voice—that is sparked by the Divine. Here is the challenge: How do you move this principle into action?

Godtalk

How does stating this belief about God affect our relationship with God? As you have learned, we have changed the way these statements have been written from the third person (He) to the second person (You). Perhaps Maimonides used the royal third person but expected people to address these statements directly to God. As an alternative, Maimonides was simply making statements about God, rather than speaking directly to God. Does this distinction make a difference? Here is how to test it. Before addressing any prayers, choose one of the principles of faith that you have learned, and state it. Then, recite the appropriate prayer or blessing. Then, reflect on what transpired. Did things change in the context of your relationship with God?

What Can We Believe?

Is it difficult to believe in a God that is beyond our human comprehension? It would be much easier if we could point to a God that you could see or feel or touch. Remember the midrash about Abraham in his father Terach's idol shop? Many Jews don't even realize that it this not part of the Torah story since it is repeated so frequently. It seems that, one day, Abraham was left in charge of his father's idol shop. While his father was gone, Abraham smashed all of the idols. When his father returned and had surveyed the damage, he asked his son what had happened. Abraham explained that this idol had smashed that one. And that one had smashed this one. His father reprimanded him, "Son, don't you know that they are just wood and stone? How can you tell me that they are capable of doing that to one another?" Finally, Terach realized the religious truth that his son had taught him.

Abraham knew about faith. He experienced it. It is a feeling that is difficult to articulate, hard to put into words. That is one of the things the Torah tries to do for us by telling us about the struggles of our ancestors. But we have to eventually come to it on our own. Faith is that feeling that we encounter deep within the recesses of our souls. Can you try to describe it?

_____

_____

_____

_____

The Spectrum of Jewish Belief: Reform, Conservative, and All the Rest

On this principle there is no disagreement among the various religious movements in Judaism.

PRINCIPLE FOUR

The Beginning and the End

I believe with perfect faith that the Creator, praised be Your name, is the first and the last.

Getting Started: Some Background

This is a difficult principle. It is filled with more mental gymnastics in the form of Godtalk and theology than the other principles. As a result, you may want to skip over it and come back to it once you are more comfortable with the rest of the material in this volume. Alternatively, you may want to review the material on this principle more quickly than you have that of previous principles.

Before we begin an in-depth analysis of this statement, write down what you think Maimonides meant to say when he wrote it—and why he included this idea as one of his thirteen principles. Then, after you have concluded your work on this chapter, come back to what you have written and make any necessary changes. The development of theology in this way is what scholars call "construct theology." Feel free to ask others to offer an opinion on it. Perhaps you may want to compare the answers of a parent or grandparent to your own.

_____

_____

_____

_____

This principle has two foci: the eternal nature of God, and the uniqueness of God in regard to that eternalness. Additionally, just as in the first three principles, God is called the Creator in this principle too. (As a matter of fact, Maimonides refers to God as Creator in eight of the thirteen principles.) According to Maimonides, God's primary function appears to be as Creator. God's ability to create and God's position as the Creator of the world are affirmed by this principle. One might even say that one emerges out of the other. In order to make this claim, Maimonides has to make sure that the way in which he conceptualizes God is beyond the claims of all other religions. In this fourth principle of faith, Maimonides takes the perspective of time and describes the superlative character of God (unmatched to anything) as well. First, nothing has come before and nothing will come after God. As a result, everything that comes in between is in a relationship with God, because God brought it all into being. Second, nothing has or will supersede the Divine.

It seems like the only thing theologians really want to do is talk about God. Everything else is nearly irrelevant because it all pales in comparison to God. Why do you think these ideas are important to Judaism, and why does Maimonides believe they are central to Jewish belief?

A Ready Reference

The eternal nature of God: We are not able to comprehend the eternal nature of God. The idea of eternality (in time and in space) extends beyond the scientific notion that we live in a perpetually expanding universe. The conclusion to its history (the recording of events over time) emerges with the coming of the Messiah (see principle 12).

The uniqueness of God in regard to that eternalness: Because nothing else can claim such extensive eternality, nothing else can be compared to God.

What We Believe

How do we make sense out of this theology, much of which seems rather distant from our daily lives? While we do not want to say that it is irrelevant, this principle of Maimonides seems totally unrelated to the challenges of daily living. Martin Buber, the theologian and philosopher who taught us about "I-Thou" relationships, also taught us about the dual nature of our faith. This is where the relevance of the fourth principle enters the discussion. Buber argued that there is a large part of faith that is an inheritance from our ancestors. Our ancestors struggled through lots of ideas before handing them down to us. We learn it from parents and teachers and accept it just as we accept other truths from them. It is part of our relationship with those whom we respect and trust. That's why the chain of Jewish tradition (called *shalshelet ha-kabbala* in Hebrew) is so important.

A strictly inherited faith was insufficient for Buber. He believed that our faith demanded more from us. Buber suggested that we also reason about religious ideas on our own. This combination of ancestral faith and faith derived from our own reason will lead us to a more secure and profound faith.

Make a list of some of the things that might be considered part of the ancestral faith that you have inherited from parents and teachers. (Is this principle among them?)

1. _____
2. _____
3. _____
4. _____
5. _____
6. _____
7. _____
8. _____
9. _____
10. _____

Now, go back to your list, and consider which elements you are prepared to accept based on your own reasoning. Circle those which you want to affirm (or *confirm*). Feel free to use an additional sheet of paper as a worksheet or to add to your list. Then, add any additional items that you have come to understand on your own about God or Judaism that you did not "inherit" from parents or teachers. Remember to include any elements relevant to Maimonides' fourth principle of faith.

1. _____
2. _____
3. _____
4. _____
5. _____

An Exercise

The next time you are in the synagogue, pay close attention to the Adon Olam prayer. As you know, this is the song that generally concludes Saturday morning worship. It sometimes is sung on Friday night as well. For many on Saturday morning, it is a signal for people to remove their *tallitot* or even start a recession to the exit of the *bet knesset*. Others use it as a game of sorts, for it has been sung to more melodies than probably any other piece of Jewish liturgy. As a result, its principles are often lost. Take a look at the last line of the song, one of the most powerful ideas in the entire service—and it is usually lost to the shuffling of feet, the closing of books, and just a general lack of attention. The text can be loosely translated as "As long as God is with me, I am not afraid."

Maimonides' fourth principle is contained in Adon Olam as well. But it may not be written in words with which you are familiar. In S.A.T. fashion, see if you can explain the text as it is written in Adon Olam, and then, try to explain its relationship to the fourth principle.

Extending the Principle of Faith

Often Jewish folk music reflects fundamental Jewish beliefs that we often take for granted or overlook while we are singing. One such case involves a liturgical text and is usually just referred to by the first word *Emet* (truth). The song text is as follows:

Emet (repeated 9 times) *ata hu rishon.*
Emet (repeated 9 times) *ata hu acharon*
Umebaladekha, ain lanu melekh. goel umoshiah (line repeated twice).
It is true that You are the first.
It is true that You are the last.
Besides You, we have no Sovereign Ruler, Redeemer, nor Savior.

How are such songs used as a means of affirming one's faith?

Personalizing the Principle of Faith

How does the acknowledgment of this principle affect my religious life, if at all? And, is my religious belief system challenged if I cannot accept this particular principle? These are the basic questions that each of us must ask of ourselves after reading and reflecting on this principle (and others). Now comes the challenge of confirmation. If I accept this principle, how do I make it part of my religious life? Some suggest that we simply place ideas like this in our regular prayers. See if you can find this statement (even poetically described) in the *siddur*. But that makes it too easy. How else can we take hold of this idea?

Textual Encounters
Text I:

Your teaching is true and enduring. Your words are established forever. They are awesome and revered, eternally right. They are well-ordered and always acceptable. They are sweet, precious, good, beautiful, and beloved. It is true that the eternal God is our Sovereign; the Rock of Jacob is our protecting shield. God is eternal, and God's Presence is eternal. God is for all generations, and God's throne is firmly established. God's faithfulness endures for all time.

(From the paragraph following the Shema)

Why does this paragraph follow the line in the third paragraph of the Shema, "I am Adonai who brought you out of the land of Egypt"?

Why is the eternalness of God stressed so many times in this paragraph?

Why is God called Rock? What does the word "rock" suggest concerning God's character? Where else in the prayer book or Torah is God called a rock?

What other things are eternal besides God?

Text 2:

Commenting on the verse, "There is none as God, for there is none besides You" (I Samuel 2:2), Rabbi Judah bar Menasya said, "Do not read *biltecha*. Instead, read *ballotech*—there is none that can outlive you. For the behavior of God is not like the behavior of flesh and blood. Flesh and blood: the works of human hands can outlive the human. But the Holy Blessed One, God, outlives God's works."

(Talmud, Megillah 14a)

What does it mean that God outlives God's works? In what way can or does a person's works outlive that person? Is there any way that a person can, like God, outlive his or her work? What can a person do to ensure that he or she will be remembered after death, eternally?

How Judaism Differs

For the three major monotheistic religions, it can probably be said that God is the first and the last even if God is called by different names among different faith communities. Other religions may contend that God as we conceive the divine is not the first or the last. Find out what these religions say about this idea about God.

Christianity

_____

_____

_____

Islam

_____

_____

_____

Buddhism

_____

_____

_____

From Faith to Deeds

How do we translate this principle into action? It is not an easy task. So form a *chevruta* (partnered learning) with someone else and develop a list of options together. Be prepared to explain your choices.

Godtalk

How do the Torah and Jewish tradition teach us about this principle? Well, here's one idea. One of the last things that we do before we go to sleep at night is to say the *Shema*, a declaration of faith to be said even as we drift off to sleep. The rabbis probably initiated the requirement because sleep, in an odd sort of way, simulates death. And, unfortunately, many do die during sleep. There is even a beautiful midrash that suggests that when babies go to sleep at night, God's *Shechina* actually changes places with them, and God assigns the ministering angels to watch over the infant while it is sleeping. But the *Shema* reminds and reaffirms for us that God is always there. God was there before we were born and God will be there even after we die.

What Can We Believe?

This principle probably causes us little reason to rethink our personal beliefs. It is a rather simple acknowledgment that God is God. There was nothing before God and there will be nothing after God, for God stretches before time and beyond it.

The Spectrum of Jewish Belief: Reform, Conservative, and All the Rest

While it can be said that there is nothing in this principle that separates the various religious movements, there are individual streams of thought in each of the movements which might take a different approach to this principle regardless of which movement's ideology they subscribe to. Interview a representative of a movement (rabbi, cantor, educator) other than your own. Ask them to interpret this principle in light of their own movement. Then, compare their answer to what you have learned about your own movement.

PRINCIPLE FIVE

The Direction of Prayer

I believe with perfect faith that to the Creator, praised be Your name, and to You alone, it is right to pray, and that it is not right to pray to any being besides You.

Getting Started: Some Background

Prayer is about dialogue, an ongoing conversation between God and individual human beings. Too often, we try to talk to God only when we are facing a challenge, whether the problem is physical, emotional, or spiritual. But the dialogue should emerge out of a relationship, what we call a covenantal relationship, rather than in response to a particular need. If we try to initiate that dialogue before entering into the relationship or only when we need divine assistance, we may find that we are unable to do so or that God may be unwilling to listen.

Levi Yitzchak of Berditchev, one of our favorite Hasidic rebbes, told the following story as part of his sermon on Rosh Hashanah one year:

It seems that a member of his community had lost his business in a fire. He was bemoaning his predicament at a local pub. What troubled him most was not that he had lost his business. (No insurance in those days!) He was concerned that he had purchased goods from a supplier intending to sell the goods and then pay the supplier. He still owed the money to his supplier and had no means by which to pay him. And he had no way to get additional goods to start his business once again. One of this friends suggested that he explain his predicament to the supplier. Not knowing what to expect, the storekeeper followed his friend's suggestion and walked to the edge of town where the supplier lived. Just as he prepared to knock on the door, the enormity of his problem overwhelmed him. Before he could muster the strength to knock on the door, he slumped into tears. The homeowner heard crying outside his door, and he hastened to see what was going on. When he opened the door, he saw his customer sitting on the front steps sobbing loudly. The homeowner asked what was the matter, and, amid sobs, the storekeeper told him the entire story. After pausing a moment, the storekeeper said, "Don't worry. We have been business associates for a long time. I trust you and you trust me. I will forgive your debt now, and lend you new merchandise to get you started again. Eventually you will repay me." Joyfully, the man returned to his friends at the pub, thanked his friend for encouraging him to pursue the supplier, and went home.

One of the men at the pub overheard the entire conversation and hurried home to relate the incident to his spouse. His spouse suggested that, although he did not own a store, he should try the same thing with the other man's supplier. Maybe he would lend them the money to start a business.

So he went found his way to the supplier's house and sat on the steps and cried. When the homeowner heard the commotion, he came to the front door once again to find a stranger. In a less than welcoming tone, he asked, "Who are you and what do you want?" To the question, the man told him what he had heard at the pub and thought that he might do the same for him. With that, the homeowner roared, "Get out of here. We don't know each other and you expect me to help you! How dare you!"

After telling the story, Levi Yitzchak said to the congregation, "The same can be said of you. Many of you do not have a relationship with God, and yet you come here on Rosh Hashanah and Yom Kippur expecting God to forgive you, and to enter you into the book of life for a new year."

What do you think of Levi Yitzchak's story? How does it apply to you? To your friends? To members of your family?

A Ready Reference

Most prayer can be separated into two major categories: petition or praise. A petitionary prayer asks for something. A prayer of praise simply acknowledges God for who and what God is. These prayers are either fixed (*keva* in Hebrew) or spontaneous (*kavanna* in Hebrew). If they are fixed, we can find them in the same form in the same place in most prayer books (even if they change a little over time, or among the religious movements, or even for a specific occasion). If they are spontaneous, they can emerge from the heart at any moment. The life of Jewish prayer contains opportunities for both. Sometimes one is contained in the other.

What We Believe

Usually we think that prayer does not work when we ask something of God and we do not get the answer we would like. We make the erroneous assumption that just because we ask, God has the responsibility to answer. Some believe that we cannot ask God to intervene in our lives and the workings of the world through prayer. Others believe that God is capable of intervening in our lives and in the daily life of the world.

One rabbi puts it this way: Prayer cannot bring water to parched fields, or mend a broken bridge, or rebuild a ruined city, but prayer can water an arid soul, mend a broken heart, and rebuild a weakened will.

What do you think can prayer do? Have you experienced that kind of prayer in your life?

Rabbi Mordecai Kaplan, the founder of Reconstructionism, believed in the *people* of Israel—what he liked to refer to as the folk. God could not be persuaded to intervene on a daily basis. Instead God was contained in the laws of nature, the laws that govern the natural world. So he taught that the primary function of prayer is the coming together of a community. This was very important to Kaplan, because in the synagogue Jews share their common dreams and aspirations. And when you leave worship, the ideas that were expressed are those that you should take hold of and emulate.

There is an old joke about people who talk in the synagogue during services. The punch line goes something like this: Schwartz comes to synagogue to talk to God. I come to the synagogue to talk to Schwartz.

What other reasons motivate people to come to synagogue services besides prayer? What are some of the things that motivate you to come (besides parental pressure), even if your primary reason might be to pray?

Are there other places besides the sanctuary in which you feel comfortable praying? What is it about that space that encourages prayer? Where do you go outside of the synagogue to pray? What are the things you look for in a prayer space?

In the space below, design a prayer space that speaks to your personal needs.

An Exercise

Keep a log book which records your ongoing dialogue with God. Include formal and informal prayer. After you have kept the log for two weeks, consider the pattern of your prayer life. How does it change from day to day, from week to week? Then, consciously add an element drawn from this to your prayers, either formal or informal.

By either looking in a prayer book and finding prayers that reflect what you feel or by writing your own prayers, respond with a blessing to the following:

1. You are the sole survivor of an atomic explosion. You slowly emerge from a crater, and discover one single twig with a bud on it. You realize that the twig will grow into a tree which will provide you with oxygen for life. Select a prayer—or write one of your own—that fully expresses your gratitude for survival.

2. You have just been defeated in your class representative election. You are unhappy, angry, and somewhat jealous of your opponent. You are trying your best to go on with your life. Select a prayer that might help you through this difficult time.

3. You have just learned that you have been admitted to the college of your choice. You are elated and believe that this is one of the happiest days of your life. Select a prayer—or write one of your own—that expresses your feelings.

4. You are a police officer, and have apprehended a serial killer—after a life-threatening gunfight. You bring him to the police station, and are relieved that your life has been spared. Select a prayer that expresses your feelings.

5. You are at summer camp, and have been indoors for a period of three days due to torrential rains. The rain finally abated and the sun is now shining. You go outside and see a magnificent rainbow. What prayer are you motivated to say?

6. You are at camp in northern Canada. One night, you see the sky filled with meteor showers and even the aurora borealis. You are awed by what you see. Choose a prayer that reflects your feelings.

7. You have just learned that your brother or sister has become engaged to be married. You are very happy and want to jump for joy. What prayer would best approximate your feelings at the moment?

8. Your best friend has just been diagnosed with a life-threatening disease. You learn about it from her mother, and are shocked and deeply concerned. Select a prayer that might help her (and you).

Extending the Principle of Faith

Most people believe that worship services replaced the sacrifices in the Temple. While this is true, prayer services began before the Temple was destroyed, and then fully replaced the sacrificial system following the destruction of the Temple in 70 C.E. Formal Jewish worship takes place three times a day (morning, afternoon, and evening), seven days a week.

But there are lots of opportunities for informal and spontaneous prayer. Can you name some of these opportunities? The rabbis say that we should say one hundred blessings each day—and that we should look for opportunities to recite these blessings. Two of the daily services reflect the sacrifices in the Temple, but a third one was added. In addition, the *musaf* additional service on Shabbat and festivals reflects the additional sacrifice that was offered at the Temple on those occasions. Reform Judaism rejected this additional service, because it rejected a connection to the Temple and its sacrificial system. Thus, it moved some of its liturgical embellishments into the rest of the service. This is particularly true on Rosh Hashanah where the *musaf amidah* forms an important part of the morning service. While the *musaf* service has not been reinstated, the movement has softened its position somewhat with regard to the ancient Temple.

If you were to wander into a synagogue, not knowing exactly what day it was and what to expect, you would be able to tell the day by listening to the liturgy. While the core of the service is the same, there are extra words, verses, and whole sections that are added which reflect the theme of the Sabbath and holidays. What else helps you know what service it is?

When we pray we are supposed to face Jerusalem. The *bet knesset* in our synagogues is usually set up this way. However, sometimes it is hard to know what direction is east (toward Jerusalem). When you don't know, says the medieval Jewish poet Judah Halevy, you should turn your heart to Jerusalem.

When praying at home, people place plaques on the eastern wall so that they will know which way to face when praying. This plaque is called a *mizrach*, from the Hebrew word for "east."

There is a certain rhythm to prayer. Some people experience the rhythm by swaying back and forth (this is called shuckling). It is like tapping your foot or clapping your hands to the beat of music. Here, your entire body responds to prayer. In addition, there are other things that people do as part of prayer. We like to call this the choreography (or the dance) of prayer.

Think about a recent worship service that you participated in. As you watched people stand and sit, perhaps take steps backwards and forwards and even bow occasionally, what image went through your mind? There are two templates which can be placed over the worship service that help us to understand the Jewish notion of prayer. The first is the courtroom and focuses on God as Judge. The second is the throne room in a palace and focuses on God as King (or, as we prefer to say, Sovereign Ruler).

Prayer Choreography

After reviewing the first three columns and experiencing what is described in the synagogue, fill in column four.

When	What to do	How to do it	Why
In general	Shuckling	Swaying back and forth on your feet	
Barechu	Bowing	Bow from the waist on the word *barekhu*	
Shema Yisrael Adonai Elohenu Adonai Echad	Closing your eyes	Cover your eyes with your right hand	
Third paragraph of the *Shema* (i.e., *Vayomar Adonai*)	Kissing *tzitzit* (fringes)	Gather *tzitzit* and kiss them at each mention of *tzitzit* in their paragraph of *Shema*.	
Adonai sifatai tiftach ufi yagid tihilatekha (verse before the Amida)	Approaching God	Walk back three steps and forward three steps	
Barukh ata Adonai Elohenu vaylohay (beginning of Amida)	Bowing	Bend knees at *barukh*, bend over your waist at *avotaynu ata* and straighten up at *Adonai*	

When	What to do	How to do it	Why
Barukh ata Adonai magen Avraham (v'ezrat Sarah), second blessing in the *Amida*	Bowing	Same as above	
Kedusha on the words *Kadosh, kadosh, kadosh*	Rise on tiptoes at each mention of the word *kadosh*		
Modim anachnu lakh (in *Amida*)	Bowing	Same as first blessing of *Amida*	
Barukh ata Adonai hatov shimkha ulekha na'eh lehodot (in *Amida*)	Bowing	Same as above	
Oseh shalom bimromav hu yaaseh shalom aleynu ve'al kol Yisrael veimru amen	Taking leave of God	Take three steps backward: at *shalom bimromav* bend your head and shoulders to the left; at *hu yaaseh shalom* bend your head and shoulders to the right; at *aleynu ve'al kol Yisrael* bend your head and shoulders forward; at *veimru* stand erect	
Aleynu, on words *va'anachnu korim umishtachavim umodim*	Bow	Bend knees at *va'anachnu korim*, bow at *umishtachavim*, stand erect at *lifney melekh*	

Personalizing the Principle of Faith

An important part of prayer is the music that animates it. Sometimes, prayer has a sing-song quality. This is called a prayer mode or *nusach*. If you listen carefully, you can get a sense of the spiritual character of the particular worship service by listening to the *nusach*, which is different for each kind of service. Hopefully, the music used in a particular service captures this emotion.

But there are others things to consider about the music. Cantor Benji Ellen Schiller divides the music used in services into four categories:

1. Majesty: Music that elicits the awesome nature of God.

2. Meditation: Music that encourages personal reflection.

3. Memory: Music that evokes the particular customs of a community, or provides us the path to connect with past generations.

4. Meeting: Music that promotes community. This music is easily accessible, and provides the means through which singing communities can evolve.

There has been a trend in congregations away from prayer that is led solely by the rabbi or cantor toward prayer that is totally participatory. Ideally, we believe that a worship service should contain all of these elements, but we realize that synagogues tend to be less participatory than they should be. This may alienate individuals who want to be part of a community. We are advocates of music that builds worshiping communities in which we all can participate.

Make a checklist of worship in your community. Make a list of all of the major prayers that are chanted or sung. Next to each prayer, write down the kind of music that was used (majesty, meditation, memory, meeting). Then determine what music "colors" the service. Is it mostly majestic, meditation, memory, or meeting? After you have come to a conclusion, ask participants in the service and members of the congregation who have not attended the service you are evaluating what kind of music dominates the service. Compare their answers to your conclusion. If there is a discrepancy, to what do you attribute it? What changes would you recommend to the service in order to promote community?

Textual Encounters

The shortest prayer in the entire Bible was spoken by Moses on behalf of his sister Miriam, who had contracted leprosy. The words were simple and heartfelt: *El na, refah na la,* "God, please, heal her please." (Take a look at Numbers 12:13.) The words are addressed to God, somewhat respectfully (that's the function of the Hebrew word *na*) and somewhat forcefully (that's the command form for "heal," *refah*).

Psalms are also a form of prayer. According to tradition, David chanted these psalms to King Saul in order to comfort and console him. Various selections of the psalms (in whole or in part) are used in our liturgy. Open to the Friday evening service, and see how many full psalms you encounter. Make a list of them here.

The psalms can stand on their own. They provide us with words when we don't have any left inside of us, when we aren't able to articulate what is in our heart: the burden we carry, or the joy we want to express. And in the 150th psalm, when our words fail, when we have nothing left to say, we try to speak through musical instruments. And then comes the most powerful text in the entire book of Psalms: *Kol haneshama tehallel Yah.* "Let every living being (let our very breath) praise God."

Try saying this line softly with just your breath forming the sounds of the words. Use it as a *kavanna,* or a sacred Jewish mantra. Repeat it over and over until it becomes a part of you.

God's Prayer

> Rabbi Yochanan said in the name of Rabbi Yose.... "God, the Holy Blessed One, prays.... but what is God's prayer?" Rabbi Zutra responded in the name of Rav, "[God's prayer sounds like this] May it be my will that My mercy might overcome my wrath, and My loving qualities override my strictest of traits; that I treat My children with the quality of mercy and that I always deal with them beyond the letter of the law" (Talmud, Berakhot 7a).

What do you think of Rabbi Zutra's version of God's prayer? Were you to write one for the Holy Blessed One, what might it look like?

When you have not seen a friend in twelve months, the rabbis suggest that this blessing be said, "Praised are You God, who revives the dead" (Talmud, Berakhot 58b).

Do you recognize this phrase from someplace else? Why do you think that the rabbis selected this blessing? How does it reflect the rabbinic view of friendship? Write your own blessing, the one you intend to use after seeing a friend who you have not seen in a long time.

_____

_____

_____

Rabbi Yose says, "Whoever changes the phrasing which the Sages determined for reciting blessings has not fulfilled his (or her) obligation" (Talmud, Berakhot 40).

What do you think? What if you see a rainbow in the sky and you are inspired to say a blessing—but you do not know the specific words of our tradition? What do you do in this situation?

How Judaism Differs

While other faith communities pray to God, they may do so through a mediator, such as Jesus (in Christianity). In some cases, traditional Roman Catholics may ask a saint or the Virgin Mary (the mother of Jesus) to intercede on their behalf, regarding the prayer they want God to answer.

While Judaism teaches that Jews have direct access to God and therefore pray directly to God, one member of the community leads the community in prayer (the *shaliach tzeebor*, or *shatz* for short). This individual (often the cantor) takes cognizance of the weight of this responsibility, particularly on Yom Kippur when he or she must lead the congregation in their prayers of contrition so that they may be forgiven and "written in the book of life."

Not all religions reflect the monotheism of Judaism, Christianity, and Islam. These terms are important to remember. (They are also great S.A.T. words!)

Animism

To primitive peoples, all of nature is pervaded by countless spirits, for it is not only persons or animals, but also inanimate objects that have souls or spirits in them. This view, called animism (from the Latin anima, or "soul"), is still widespread among primitive peoples today.

Moved by awe and wonder of what they experienced, certain prehistoric peoples came to conceive of the Supernatural as something alive that inhabited everything. Consequently, whatever happened became the work of spirits, and all things, dead or alive, possessed such a living force or soul. For example, there was a spirit or soul in the tiger that people hunted. There was also a spirit in stones, bushes, and grasses.

Many remnants of animism have persisted until this day. Buddhists, for example, still revere the pipal tree under which their teacher Buddha is said to have attained enlightenment. Moslems venerate a large black stone in the court of the Great Mosque in Mecca.

Polytheism

The worship of many gods and goddesses is called polytheism. By the time the urban communities developed in the river valleys of the ancient world, polytheism was already an established view. Seven thousand years ago, the Sumerians worshiped innumerable deities, including the stars and planets, sun, and moon. It is quite likely that humans first came to conceive of the Supreme Being as a sky deity. Being impressed with the ever-present heavens under whose favor or hostility one lived, it presented a mighty being to the ancient human. For several thousand years before the era of biblical prophecy was born, polytheism in one form or another was the form in which religion flourished.

It is important to note that to the polytheist, anything wonderful or mysterious was hailed as godlike. Thus, gods were often immediately invented, named for the wonderful event, and then, should the wonder disappear, so also did the god.

Polytheism was never a serious threat to normative Judaism, because it is a form of idolatry that could never be confused with biblical doctrine.

Henotheism

There was a strong tendency in polytheistic societies to recognize and exalt one of the gods above the others. In other words, there would be a chief god—the parent of all the other gods. Thus, in Greek culture, for example, Father Zeus was the chief of the gods, considered stronger and more powerful than the others.

Sometimes one god could become the personification of the national spirit of a nationalistic people. When this occurred, the people had reached what is called "henotheism" (from the Greek *henos*, "one," and *theos*, "god"). This meant that they worshiped one god while also recognizing the existence of other gods. So-called henotheists always believed that their own god would triumph and reign supreme over all of the others. (Note: Judaism's *Mi kamocha* prayer reflects this tendency: "Who is like you among the gods that are worshiped?")

Kathenotheism

There was sometimes a tendency in polytheistic cultures for a person to worship each god in turn, as if, for the duration of the worship, there were no other gods in the universe. This tendency has been called kathenotheism, literally the worship of one god at a time. Here the devotee takes each god individually and treats him or her as if he/she were the only god in the universe.

Pantheism

Pantheism (from the Greek *pantos*, "all," and *theos*, "god") is the doctrine that God is the totality of all existing things, and that these in their totality are God. God is not a personal God, nor does God command people to seek their obedience. Consequently, there are almost no instances of pure pantheism within the normative Jewish tradition.

Pantheism received classic expression in India, which made possible its popularization by later generations of Buddhists and Hindus. Pantheism has also especially appealed to mystics because they claim to experience a oneness with God. Much primitive thought is pantheistic in tendency. Some have even considered pantheism as the earliest philosophical expression of religion. Many of the Greek thinkers before Socrates, for instance, were pantheistic in outlook, regarding the universe as a living whole of which people constitute the parts.

Deism

Deists are those who discovered that the many gods were names for the One. They may see the deities as the imperfectly conceived aspects of a divinity that is personal and completely transcendent. In this view, God is not the all. God is the source of all that is not God. God has created the universe but takes no interest in it, having withdrawn Godself from the world. Deism thus eliminates all claims of divine providence, miracles, and any form of intervention by God in history. Second, deism holds that all of the essential truths about God are knowable by natural reason without any dependence on revelation. Numerous rabbinic texts attack the Greek philosophers who taught the doctrine of deism.

Dualism

Dualism is the belief in both a good god and an evil god. In the Zoroastrian religion, for example, the good god, Ahura Mazda, is opposed by the evil one, Angra Mainyu, who in later times came to be called Shaitin (Satan). These two gods are eternally at war with each other. Ahura Mazda, the good god, was believed to be responsible for creating all the good things to be found in Persia. Angra Mainyu, on the other hand, created all the bad things (disease, sickness, and so forth).

Dualism may take other forms as well. A Persian called Mani (third century C.E.) taught a dualism of spirit and matter. The soul of a person is good, but it is in bondage to the contemptible matter that is the body. Only by denying the lusts of the body can a person overcome evil and regain the good.

Dualism was the only version of polytheism that made serious inroads into the cultural world of the Jews. As a response, the Talmud and Jewish liturgy constantly challenge the heresy of dualism.

Agnosticism

T. H. Huxley coined the word "agnostic" to express his own state of mind. In his reading, he learned of the Gnostics, who had one thing in common. They all claimed a special "gnosis" (knowledge) of divine truth. Generally speaking, they were also dualists who distinguished between the spiritual world of goodness and the material world of evil. The Gnostics claimed to know more about God than most people cared to claim. Huxley, however, claimed so much less of such knowledge that he thought the term "a-gnostic" would suit him better. Agnostics have come to be known as persons who do not categorically deny the existence of God, but rather deny that people could have any knowledge of God, who is beyond the realm of human comprehension.

Theism

Theism recognizes that God transcends the universe, while at the same time, against deism, it recognizes God's immanence in the universe. It presents the paradox that God is both remote from the universe (which is the position of deists) as well as near to people, allowing them to discover God's divine values. To theists, the universe does seem to make sense, and theists see purpose in whatever direction they turn.

From Faith to Deeds

Communal prayer is a sacred drama. Some people think this means that the clergy participants are all acting and reading from a prepared script. What makes prayer a sacred drama different from theater—even great theater like the plays of William Shakespeare—is that those who attend the drama and participate in it are expected to turn the lines of the prayers they say, hear, or read into values that govern their lives.

Think back over the last prayer service you attended. Can you think of one line in particular that struck you, which might have changed how you look at something or how you acted following the service? Write down the line, where it came from in the service (if you remember), and how it made an impact on you.

_____

_____

_____

At the next service you attend, consciously choose one line on which you want to act.

Godtalk

This whole section is about talking to God. We have focused on prayer which is primarily about verbal intercourse, communication using words. But there are other ways as well. Some people think that silence is the most powerful form of prayer. Others believe that they should engage their entire body through movement (beyond *shukling*) like dance. What other forms of communicating with God are available to us? Which ones do you make use of? How?

What Can We Believe?

There are many things to consider when we talk about prayer. Often what we believe is a result of our experiences of it. Rabbi Harold Kushner, in his book, *When Bad Things Happen to Good People*, wrote that we cannot pray to God to intervene in our lives. Instead, we can only pray to God to provide us with the strength necessary to face the burdens of life. Even that is a tall order. So what do you think? How does prayer function in the lives of individuals?

The Spectrum of Jewish Belief: Reform, Conservative, and All the Rest

While the religious movements may agree with regard to prayer, there are some segments of the community that believe that there are individuals who can intercede on our behalf. Some people believe that righteous people can help have our prayers answered. As a result, in Israel, for example, groups of traditional Jews will often pray at the grave sites of certain rabbis who they believe are *tzaddikim*, or righteous people, who can assist in our prayers.

PRINCIPLE SIX

The Prophets as God's Spokespersons

I believe with perfect faith that all the words of the prophets are true.

Getting Started: Some Background

This principle of faith concerns prophecy and the prophets of Israel. It is about hearing God's voice in the world. According to Jewish tradition, prophets were a group of human beings who were prepared (called?) to receive the word of God. It's really something to think about, but it's easier to do so when we think of the prophets as a group of people who lived a long time ago. What kind of people do you think they were? Were they regular people like you and your neighbor? (Okay, so not your neighbor, how 'bout your friend down the street?) Why did God choose them in particular, and send them on a particular mission? How were they able to hear the word of God? Why don't we have prophets today (or do we)? Is it possible that you are a prophet, able to hear the word of God—and able to then do something to fix this broken world? These are some of the questions that you are probably asking; we think about them a lot too.

Whether you realize it or not, if you have already celebrated your Bar or Bat Mitzvah, then the words of the prophets have played a significant role in your lives. You may not have realized their impact at the time, because you were busy worrying about lots of others things, like your party, friends, family, and gifts. Your Haftarah portion was taken from one of the books of the prophets from the Bible. Each Haftarah portion was chosen because it was somehow linked to the Torah portion also read during your Bar/Bat Mitzvah. So here's your first challenge: Find your Haftarah portion. What was it's main message (and how did it relate to the Torah portion)? Why was it chosen at all? And don't forget to write down whose words they were (which prophet)? Then, share the message of the prophet with your classmates.

The second section of the Hebrew Bible, the *Tanakh*, is called *Neviim*, the Hebrew word for "prophets." It begins at the time when the Judges ruled Israel. Then it traces the history of Israel's kings, commencing with Saul, and ends with the return of our ancestors from the Babylonian Exile (that's the time when we were forced to leave Israel and go to Babylonia, after the first Temple in Jerusalem was destroyed). But most important of all, this section of the Bible deals with the great literary prophets who brought the word of God to an often erring people. These are the major prophets (with big books and big messages): Isaiah, Jeremiah, and Ezekiel. The minor (sometimes called lesser) prophets are a larger group of guys. They include Hosea, Joel, Amos, Obadiah, Jonah, Micah, Nahum, Habakkuk, Zephaniah, Haggai, Zechariah, and Malachi. They too have large messages, but their books were much smaller.

All of these prophets were persons chosen by God, dedicated to bringing God's message to the world. Generally, they were called during a political or social crisis in the community. Their task was usually the same: to warn the Israelites, to counsel them, to tell them that if they did not change what they were doing and the way they were doing it, then they would be in for terrible times. See, the prophets were prophets because they were able to envision, with a little help from God, where these practices would lead the Jewish people. Fearlessly, they spoke out and criticized the lack of morality and ethics, urging the people to raise themselves up to a nobler way of living.

> **A Ready Reference**
>
> Note: *Dating before the common era (B.C.E.) seems like it runs backwards, compared to the common era (C.E.) dating to which we are accustomed.*

Elijah (early to mid-ninth century B.C.E.): Champion of God against Baal, or idol worship. He opposed Jezebel, the foreign wife of King Ahab, who introduced idol worship.

Elisha (early to mid-ninth century B.C.E): Successor of Elijah. He played an important part of the revolution against Ahab.

Jonah (early eighth century B.C.E.): Made his famous trip to Nineveh to prophesy its doom. At first, he tried to run away from God (that's how he got the name "the reluctant prophet") and so was swallowed by a big fish or, as some say, wound up "in the belly of a beast."

Amos (early to mid-eighth century B.C.E.): The prophet of justice—or doom, as he was also called—preached about the restoration and future glory of King David's kingdom

Hosea (middle to late eighth century B.C.E.): He was the prophet of love and forgiveness. His message contained the teaching of a universal God for all nations.

Isaiah (early to late eighth century B.C.E.): The statesman prophet, described the golden age of human beings. In his book, the collective Israel was described as a suffering servant.

Micah (early to late eighth century B.C.E.): Urged each person to do justice, love mercy, and walk humbly with God.

Zephaniah (late seventh century B.C.E.): He lived in the days of King Josiah's restoration, when the scroll of Deuteronomy "was discovered." He condemned strongly the idolatrous nations, and threatened God's impending judgment.

Nachum (late seventh century B.C.E.): He foretold the destruction of Sennacherib's army.

Jeremiah (late seventh to early sixth century B.C.E.): He was the prophet of sorrow. He witnessed the destruction of the ancient Temple in Jerusalem.

Habakkuk (late seventh to early sixth century B.C.E.): He preached the message of faith. God's punishment of Israel taught that "the righteous shall live by faith."

Obadiah (early sixth century B.C.E.): He directed his words against Israel's enemy, the nation called Edom. His book is only one chapter, the shortest of all the literary prophets.

Ezekiel (early sixth century B.C.E.): He was the leader and comforter of Israel while in Babylonian exile. He laid the foundation for the Jewish religion as we know it today.

Zechariah (early sixth to late sixth century B.C.E.): He is the prophet of exile who foretold the restoration of Israel and the coming of God's universal reign.

Haggai (late sixth century B.C.E.): He returned to Palestine from Babylonia and urged the people to rebuild the Temple

Malachi (middle fifth century B.C.E.): He prophesied that Elijah would announce the coming of the Messiah. His book is the last of the minor prophets in the Hebrew Bible.

Joel (fifth century B.C.E.): He lived during a plague of locusts which he interpreted as a result of God's judgment against the people. The time of his prophetic activity is uncertain.

Early Prophets in the Bible

A variety of figures in the Bible were referred to as prophets. Abraham was called a prophet:

You must restore the man's wife—since he is a prophet. (Genesis 20:7)

Moses was called a prophet twice in the Bible:

God will raise up for you a prophet from among your own people like myself. And you shall heed him. (Deuteronomy 18:15)

Never again did there arise in Israel a prophet like Moses, who God singled out, face to face. (Deuteronomy 34:10)

According to the Book of Deuteronomy, the origin of the office of prophecy is rooted in the experience at Mount Sinai. Since the Israelites were afraid of receiving God's word directly in a public revelation, they requested that Moses "go closer, and hear all that God says, and tell it to us" (Deuteronomy 5:24). This is corroborated by the following personal description of Moses: "I stood between God and you at that time to convey God's word to you, for you were afraid of the fire and did not go up the mountain" (Deuteronomy 5:5). Thus Moses became the spokesperson for God to the people. Although Moses was a person who certainly spoke for God in a special way, he is still associated more as a facilitator in the dissemination of God's Law and as a leader of the Israelites, rather than as a prophet in the more traditional sense.

The word "prophet" has had a variety of meanings during different periods of Jewish history. Some of the earliest prophets in the Bible are referred to by four different names in Hebrew: *chozeh* and *ro'eh*, both meaning "seer"; *ish ha-Elohim*, "man of God"; and *navi*, "prophet." A seer was a person who possessed the abilities to reveal information that was concealed from ordinary human beings and to foretell the future.

The term *ro'eh* is first applied to Samuel in I Samuel 9, when Saul, in search of his father's donkeys, seeks the aid of the seer Samuel, and is even prepared to pay a fee of one-quarter of a shekel. Samuel, who in this narrative (I Samuel 9:6) is also called a "man of God" and who had been previously informed by God of Saul's arrival, provides the necessary information, and, in addition, anoints Saul king of Israel. He then informs Saul of the events which are about to befall him on his way home, including the fact that he will meet a band of prophets. King Saul himself, upon the urging of Samuel the Priest, is described (I Samuel 10:5–11) as having participated in a band of roving *neviim*. In other places in the Bible, there are also references to groups of prophets, often prophesying in a state of great emotional frenzy. Such prophetic groups were often consulted for advice and asked to deliver oracles in the name of God.

The title *chozeh* is first applied to Gad in II Samuel 24:11, where Gad is called the *chozeh* of David. In essence, Gad was one of a number of court prophets who served the king. He was not a literary prophet, but a diviner, a visionary of sorts, who perhaps had some special power, and appeared to speak in God's name. He was kept in the king's court, and used to consult oracles or to make divinations, an especially important task before a major military campaign. Others were Aspah, Heman, and Jeduthun, who could prophesy with lyres, harps, and cymbals (I Chronicles 25:1ff).

These early prophets certainly played a role in the communal affairs of the Israelites. They had a number of common characteristics, including the ability to predict the future, functioning as part of a guild, employing musical accompaniment to induce or heighten their frenzy, and usually telling the people (unlike the literary prophets) what they wanted to hear.

On occasion these early prophets showed more independence and a great deal of courage. For instance, Elijah the prophet's condemnation of King Ahab over the incident of Naboth's vineyard (I Kings 21) was an act of great courage on his part, as was attacks on Baal worship. Clearly, he risked his life in standing up for what he believed to be a desecration to God. Elisha was faithful to the legacy of Elijah his master. He was forceful and often carried out his prophetic mission to perfection, even when it involved deep internal conflicts.

Sometimes the early prophets were even paid for their work. This would have been unthinkable for one of the literary prophets. Amos (7:14) denied that he was originally a prophet by profession. Micah (2:5–6) disdained prophets who made a living off of prophecy. They never reached the prominent stature of the great major and minor literary prophets whose mission always consisted of reproving the people in an attempt to save them from destruction.

Women Prophets

Five women are called prophets in the Bible. Three of them, Deborah, Huldah, and Noadiah, actually spoke in the name of God, but only Deborah and Huldah had their words recorded in the Bible. Of the remaining two, one was never identified by name and the other never prophesied.

Deborah, unlike other great women in the Bible, who are either married to a great man or related to one, stands on her own merits. She is referred to as both a military leader and as a prophetess. Together with Barak she led the Israelites in a victorious battle against the Canaanites, memorializing the victory in the "Song of Deborah" recorded in chapter 5 of the Book of Judges. A special Sabbath, known as the Sabbath of the Song, recalls the exodus from Egypt, on which we read the famous Song of Moses. (Exodus 15). On that same Sabbath, Deborah's thanksgiving song is recited as the prophetic Haftarah reading of that day, thus preserving its memory each and every year.

Huldah lived during the last years of the Judean monarchy, some five hundred years after Deborah. She predicts, in II Book of Kings, the destruction of the kingdom of Judah.

Mentioned is made in the Book of Isaiah (8:3) of the wife of the prophet Isaiah who bore him a son: "I was intimate with the prophetess, and she conceived, and bore a son." Presumably, she had claim to the title of prophetess as the wife of a well-known one.

Noadiah, sometimes referred to as the "false prophetess," is mentioned in the Book of Nehemiah (6:14) as one of a group of people who were opposed to his activities in the holy city of Jerusalem.

Lastly, Miriam, the sister of Aaron and Moses, received the title of prophetess in Exodus 15:20 upon leading the women in song and dance after the Israelites crossed the Red Sea.

Compared to their male counterparts, these women did not function as prophets in the traditional sense. They did not preach lengthy messages, nor did they have visions and dreams with which to help them predict future events for the Jewish people.

False Prophets

If you had lived in biblical times, how could you have been sure if you encountered a prophet whether that prophet was a real and authentic one? After all, in all professions in life there are reputable people as well as frauds. The description of the place of the Israelite prophets is preceded in the Bible by a stern and detailed denunciation of any dealings with people who attempt to learn the future and prophesy using means such as augury and sorcery rather than direct communication from God. Practitioners of the science of divination (including astrology, charms, incantations, and magic) were well known in the ancient Near East. Because of its popularity, the Bible cautioned strongly against its use. For example, the Book of Leviticus (19:31) warns, "Do not turn to ghosts or inquire of familiar spirits." One of the most comprehensive prohibitions occurs in Deuteronomy (18:10–12): "Let no one among you be found who consigns his son or daughter to the fire, or who is an auger, a soothsayer, a diviner, a sorcerer, or one who casts spells, or who consults ghosts or familiar spirits, or who inquires of the dead. Such a person that does these things is an abomination to God." This injunction is leveled mainly against the divinatory practices of the Canaanites, who rely too much on their own human skill to penetrate the divine mysteries. Thus divination is pagan in origin, and its practitioners continue to be linked to false prophets in various Books of the Prophets.

Interestingly, there is no Hebrew term in the Bible for a false prophet. Both false and true ones were called *neviim*–prophets. The Book of Deuteronomy attempts to provide the criteria for distinguishing a true from a false prophet immediately following its antidivination statements cited above. It says that "any prophet who presumes to speak in God's name an oracle which God did not command or speaks in the name of other gods, that prophet shall die. And should you ask yourselves, 'How can we know that the oracle was not spoken by God?' If the prophet speaks in the name of God and the oracle does not come true, that oracle was not spoken by God…" (Deuteronomy 18:20–22). In other words, the test of a true prophet is whether the prediction does or does not come true.

The next section of this chapter will describe the so-called literary prophets who had whole books filled with their words. Of all of the major prophets who wrote the largest books with the longest messages, the prophet Jeremiah is the most consistent in making speeches that are intended to combat false prophets. In his twenty-third chapter, Jeremiah, in recognizing Hananiah as a false prophet, identifies three characteristics of the false prophet:

1. Those who have dreams, and mislead people.

2. Those who "steal" God's words, and pretend that they have had a direct revelation.

3. Those who concoct their own oracles and pass them off as prophecy.

Technical expertise on the part of the people to predict the future is not and can never be true prophecy. For prophecy to be authentic the initiative must be taken entirely by God, who communicates intentions through visions, and cannot be coerced by any humanly devised means, no matter how clever, to reveal God's designs.

After Prophecy: The *Bat Kol*

With the deaths of Malachi, Zechariah, and Haggai in the fifth century B.C.E., the classical literary prophets come to an end. According to rabbinic tradition, the *bat kol*, a heavenly voice became the sole mechanism by God to reveal God's will to human beings after the cessation of prophecy (Talmud, Yoma 9b). The rabbis believed that the *bat kol* was already heard during biblical times. For instance, in the Talmud (Makkot 23b), they believed that it was heard to proclaim Tamar's innocence, as well as to validate Solomon's judgment in awarding the child to the true mother. In the Midrash, a *bat kol* also tells Moses that God will attend the burial of Moses.

The *bat kol* was sometimes said to give heavenly approval to Jewish legal decisions, although its pronouncements were not necessarily accepted.

What We Believe

The notion of Jewish prophecy is based on one premise: God chooses to make the divine will known to certain individuals in successive generations. These individuals, called prophets, are described as charismatic people endowed with a divine gift: They can receive divine revelation and then teach what has been revealed to them. Even when they disagreed with the message or even did not want to deliver it, prophets were compelled to do so.

But how did God speak to the prophets? How were they able to hear what God was saying? Did they have to train themselves (or get training from someone else)? Were they born with a special faculty, a special sense? What does it mean when the Bible says that God "spoke" to the prophet? Should we take such statements literally or symbolically? In other words, did God not actually speak, but it was as if God had spoken? What would the divine voice sound like to a prophet? And how can we be sure (and this goes for the prophets themselves) that the words they heard were real, that their so-called prophetic experience was a valid one? Could their words be verified?

Throughout the Bible, God frequently speaks to specific individuals. For example, we often read that "God spoke thus to Moses" as a way of introducing a dialogue that takes place between God and Moses. Likewise, God spoke to the prophets. They did not attempt to speak to God before God had spoken to them. It even seems as if God searched out people to be prophets rather than that the prophets were groping for God.

And, if God spoke during the time of the Bible, why doesn't God speak to us today in the same compelling way? Maybe God is still speaking; it's just that there is just too much noise today for us to hear God's voice.

Jewish tradition suggests that the ability to hear God's voice depends on the individual. In order to "hear" God one must have a strong will and use all of one's heart and mind to discern God's voice. One must make a strong effort to "hear" God by beginning with this question of self-scrutiny: "What does God require of me?"

The great prophets of Israel perceived God everywhere: in the wind, in the rushing waters, in the fiery flame, in the desert sands. Don't count on science to explain how or what God hears. It is impossible to pierce the mystery, although we can be awed by it. Arno Penzias, the scientist who who described primary evidence for the Big Bang and was a winner of the 1978 Nobel Prize, once said that science only describes; it does not try to explain or understand. Only religion attempts to do so.

In the Book of Kings (there are two volumes because the original scrolls were rather large and therefore divided into two), the prophet Elijah finds himself on top of a mountain. There he experiences fire, earthquake, and wind. Take a look at the nineteenth chapter of the First Book of Kings. We find that the Bible tells us that God is not expressed primarily in the roaring fire, the trembling earthquake and the force of wind—as we might expect. Rather, God is found in "the still, small voice" (I Kings 19:12). It is here that Elijah learned the importance of silence and listening. Perhaps we too need to be better listeners, waiting for God to draw us closer with the silent voice.

Extending the Principle of Faith

According to Moses Maimonides (the author of the thirteen principles of faith that we are studying), prophecy rests on the wise person who is distinguished by strong moral character. Centuries ago, he wrote, "The prophets are of various degrees. Just as one sage is greater in wisdom than another, so too in the gift of prophecy is one prophet greater than another" (*Yesodei ha-Torah* 7:2). He further writes that "everyone should be a prophet, who is well-built physically and has been duly educated and trained . . . fools and ignorant people are not fit for this distinction . . .

prophecy is impossible without study and training" (*Guide for the Perplexed* 2:32). What is your opinion of what Maimonides had to say? Is it possible for people today to be trained to become prophets?

One thing is clear from the prophets who wrote their words in books: They were people dedicated to God's service, who sought God's guidance. In the light of revelation the prophet pondered the problems of the Jewish people.

Over the centuries, Jewish philosophers have debated the role of prophecy and the essence of the Jewish prophet. While some have treated prophecy as a subjective experience (i.e., a form of psychological delusion), others have regarded the message of the prophet as the authentic disclosure of a message received word for word from God.

Abraham Joshua Heschel, a great modern Jewish philosopher, liked to tell the following story from the Hasidic tradition, which is attributed to the Baal Shem Tov. A musician was playing on a very beautiful instrument, and the music so captivated the people that they were driven to dance ecstatically. Then a deaf person—who knew nothing of music passed by. Seeing the enthusiastic dance of the people, he decided that they must be insane. Had he been wise, he would have sensed their joy and joined in the dancing.

We cannot hear the voice. But when we read carefully, we can see the words of the prophets. Even when we are deaf, we will then be able to see the rapture of their words.

Personalizing the Principle of Faith

It is now your turn to try to formulate your own personal beliefs relating to Jewish prophets and prophecy. Remember that Jewish faith is never without doubt, questioning, or challenge.

1. Do you believe that prophecy is a fundamental principle of Judaism?

2. How would you define the word "prophet"? Do you believe that each prophet heard the word of God as each describes it in writing?

3. Can you or I be a prophet? What conditions must be met before we accept someone as a prophet?

4. What do you think are the greatest achievements of the Jewish prophets?

5. Who is your favorite prophet, and why?

6. Who do you think is Judaism's greatest prophet?

7. How would you rate the prophets as teachers of the people?

8. Some people have considered persons such as Martin Luther King, Jr. to be a prophet, although he never called himself a prophet in the biblical sense. Do you have any candidates (persons now living or in the recent past) who you believe meet the certain characteristics that were associated with the biblical prophets of the ancient past? Who are they, and why did you choose them?

9. Why do you believe that the message of the biblical prophets has survived until modern times? What do their words mean to us today?

10. How do you think the prophets of Israel would have responded to some of the conditions in today's society? If they could speak to us today, what would they say? What would they criticize? .

11. Would you have wanted to have been a prophet in Israel?

12. What is the single most important piece of advice that you have discovered or been taught in one of the books of the prophets?

13. Who are your role models today, the heroes (men and women) whom you want to most like? What are their values? Can you imagine a person living at the time of the Bible who might want to use one of the prophets as a role model? Is there a prophet who you have studied whom you would want to use as a personal role model? What is your reason for your choice?

14. Imagine that you were a prophet, and had to make a speech to the people warning them of the hazards of smoking. Choose a partner and play the role of the prophet, trying to convince him/her (who will represent the Jewish people) that smoking is the wrong thing to do, and is antithetical to God's instruction "choose life."

15. If the prophets were alive today, what do you think they would say about the following:
   a. using drugs
   b. capital punishment
   c. violence and terrorism
   d. abortion
   e. physician-assisted suicide

16. In the Midrash (Numbers Rabbah 14) the rabbis state: "In this world, only individuals were prophets. In the next world, all Israel will be prophets." What do you think is meant by this statement? Do you agree or disagree with it?

17. According to another midrash (Shocher Tov), all prophets open their speeches with a reprimand (that's what your parents do when they want you to behave) and end with soft words of comfort and consolation. Do you agree with this approach? What can we learn about our relationships with others from this approach?

18. Abraham Joshua Heschel once wrote (in a book called *God in Search of Man*, p. 255), "The word was not given to the prophets for their own sake. We were all faced by God when the prophets were faced by Him. We are all addressed, when the prophets were spoken to. Our faith is derived from our *perceptiveness to the word that has gone out to all of us*." What is your reaction to this statement? Do you agree or disagree with it? Why do you think that God needed prophets?

19. Do you believe with perfect faith in the principle that "all of the words of the prophets are true?"

Textual Encounters

Here are some passages taken directly from the books of the Prophets. Each deals with a belief or value that was espoused by that particular prophet. After reading each passage, try to answer the questions that follow. It will offer you a chance to analyze your beliefs as they relate to those of the prophets:

Text I:

You alone have I singled out of all the families of the earth. This is why I will call you to account for all of your iniquities.

(Amos 3:2)

Questions:

How does this passage help us to understand Amos' view of Jews as the chosen people?

Do you believe that you are a chosen person? If so, how does this belief translate into things that you do in your life? How does the concept of chosenness relate to your commitment to Jewish study in Confirmation class?

Is it possible for God to have a treasured people?

Text 2:

God has told you, O man, what is good, and what God requires of you: Do justly, love mercy, and walk humbly with your God?
(Micah 6:8)

Questions:

What do you believe that God requires of you?

How would you define a person who does things justly? What kind of a person is a lover of mercy?

Do you agree with Micah that humility is a virtue?

Text 3:

What need do I have of frankincense that comes from Sheba/ Or fragrant cane from a distant land?/ Your burnt offerings are not acceptable/ And your sacrifices are not pleasing to Me.
(Jeremiah 6:20)

Questions:

Why do you think Jeremiah is disgusted with the ritual practices described in the above passage?

What rituals do you find meaningful in your life? Are there any rituals that are not acceptable to you or the meaning of which you have difficulty in discerning?

Text 4:

Not by might, nor by power, but by My spirit, says *Adonai Tzevaot* [the God of Hosts].
(Zechariah 4:6)

Questions:

What is your opinion of a person who claims the status of a conscientious objector and chooses not to serve in the armed forces of a country? Can a Jew be a conscientious objector? Can a Jew be a pacifist?

Text 5:

Return, O Israel to Adonai your God./ For you have stumbled in your iniquity./ Take with you words/ and return to God.

(Hosea 14:2–3)

Questions:

From this verse, how do you understand the prophet Hosea's concept of repentance in relation to God? Do you agree with his understanding of *teshuva*?

What are some ways of showing that you have returned to God? How do you make amends to God on the High Holy Days?

Text 6:

I shall betroth you to Me forever/ I shall betroth you to Me with righteousness and justice, with love and mercy/ I shall betroth you to Me in truth, and you shall know God.

(Hosea 2:21–22)

Questions:

Some people have said that the above words by Hosea are his way of defining the covenant between God and Israel. If so, what is Hosea's definition of a covenant?

In what ways is one's relationship to God like a marriage? What are some things that one can learn from a good marriage that would help a person better his/her relationship with God?

How Judaism Differs

Do you believe that Jesus or Mohammed was a prophet in the Jewish sense?

We now should have a better concept of what a Jewish prophet is and is not. Perhaps you have asked: Have there been prophets since the days of the biblical prophets? Was Mohammed, the founder of Islam, a prophet? Muslims certainly believe so. Some Christians believe that Jesus was a prophet, although many more consider him to be divine.

Jews do not consider Jesus to be a prophet. For one thing, Jesus in a number of places in the New Testament prefers to think of himself as divine, and no prophet of Israel would have dared thought of making this kind of claim. The prophets used the formula, "Thus says the Lord Adonai . . ." but Jesus said, "You have heard it said . . ." This is not prophet talk in Jewish terms.

> When Jesus came into the district of Caesarea Philipi, he asked his disciples, "Who do men say that I the Son of man am?" And they said, "Some say John the Baptist, others say Elijah, and others Jeremiah, or one of the prophets." He said to them, "But who do you say that I am?" Simon Peter replied, "You are the Christ, the Son of the living God." And Jesus answered, "Blessed are you . . ."
> (Matthew 16:13–17)

For many Jews who have ever taken the time to think about their beliefs concerning Jesus, they would probably consider him a charismatic teacher rather than a prophet of God.

For Christians, the death and resurrection of Jesus are more important than his life. According to Christianity, it is through his death that humankind is redeemed from sin. It has never been a Jewish tenet that the death of a prophet is intended to serve a redemptive purpose.

There are people who believe that new prophets have arisen since biblical times and continue to do so. Perhaps you do too. Charismatic leaders and teachers who buck the status quo, such as Martin Luther King, Jr. or Mohandas Gandhi, have been seen as prophets in their own day, although these men have never called themselves prophets in the Jewish sense. Although they shared some of the characteristics of true prophets, such as their concern for combating societal evils and an ability to passionately speak and write about their feelings, they clearly cannot be considered prophets in the biblical sense. Unlike the biblical prophets, these men did not represent themselves as personally speaking in the name of God. The prophets, on the other hand, would often introduce their speeches as "the word of God came to me, saying . . ." They were chosen by God and spoke in God's name.

This does not mean that people today cannot bear attributes that resemble those of the prophets of bygone days. Certainly our world today is filled with enough evils, ills, and social injustices that yearn to be fixed, and there is need for proactive leaders to speak out for change and improvement. Judaism has always stressed the ethic of social justice, and the Torah commands, "justice, justice shall you pursue" (Deuteronomy 16:20). When Abraham believed God was acting inappropriately, he confronted God with a stark challenge: "Will the Judge of all the earth not act with justice?" (Genesis 18:25). For the prophets justice is what most mattered to God. "Let justice well up as waters, and righteousness as a mighty stream" declares the prophet Amos in what is the most oft-quoted verse from his book (5:24).

From Faith to Deeds

The prophets ought to continue to serve as true models for us today. The struggle to refine the world is a desperately important one. Jews to this day have persisted in believing in their divinely appointed role to bring all people to the recognition of God's moral standard. Each one of us is called upon to listen for that *bat kol*, the divine voice that reminds us of our mission: To serve, in the ancient words of the prophet Isaiah, as "a light unto the nations."

Godtalk

According to Jewish tradition, God charged the prophet with the responsibility of carrying the divine message to the people. The Torah tells us that God only spoke to Moses *panim el panim*, or face to face. To the other prophets God spoke in dreams, visions, and the like.

What Can We Believe?

Prophets shared many attributes. Listed below are some of the things that characterized Jewish prophets. After you have read through them, try the exercise which follows the list. You must match the passage from the various books of the prophets with the shared characteristic.

1. Generally speaking, prophets were loners, solitary figures who did not have many close friends. Since their prediction (prophecy) generally involved something that people did not want to hear, they were unpopular, and were often denounced by the people whose lives they tried to change. This often caused them a great deal of personal pain. Interestingly, none of the prophets really wanted to be a prophet at first. This is not surprising. Would you want to have to tell people things that they were really not prepared to hear?

2. Prophets always arose at a time of social and political crisis. They would usually see their prophecy in a dream or as a night vision, or even during the day in a trancelike state.

3. All true prophets were able to correctly predict what would happen to the people of Israel. Their predictions were not grounded in reading tarot cards or crystal balls. Instead, their predictions were reflections of what God had told them, as was their revealing of what was actually happening in society.

4. Prophets would often present their messages in the form of an allegory. The interpretation of the allegory would be quickly implanted in the prophet's mind, and thus the prophet would be able to explain its meaning.

5. Prophecy was often a traumatic experience. The prophet's limbs might tremble, and the prophet might become faint.

6. Prophets often wrote down their words in books that have been named in their memory. Some prophets had scribes or secretaries to whom they dictated messages.

7. The words of the prophets were often expressive. Their message was expressed in beautiful poetry that was majestic. Because of this language, their words elicited a great deal of emotion on the part of the reader.

8. One of the tasks of the prophet was to soothe the Israelite people and provide comfort to them. The Haftarot which are selected from the books of the prophets often provide such consolation when the description of our history, as recorded in the Torah or as it is recalled on a specific holiday, requires such consolation. The Haftarot for the seven weeks after *Tisha B'av* (late July, early August) are even called the "Haftarot of Consolation."

9. Many of the things that horrified the prophets occur all over the world today.

10. Prophets were often angry with people who kept the "form" of Judaism by supporting the ancient Temple and making appropriate sacrifices but ignored ethical and moral issues, such as the plight of the poor and the hungry.

11. One major message of the prophets was about *teshuva*. God gives us a second chance by allowing us to repent for our mistakes.

12. Many of the prophets preached messages related to the importance of being a good people.

13. Prophets did not volunteer for their mission. Their mission was forced upon them; they had no choice but to do what they were asked to do.

14. Revelation, God's word (and often God's voice) came as a surprise to the prophets. Thus, they were generally startled when they heard it.

Now that you have learned what animated the prophecy of the ancient Hebrew prophets, what do you believe about these individual prophets, and the nature of prophecy itself? Does God continue to use humans as spokespersons, sent to do missions on God's behalf? What would you do if God appeared and instructed you to go on a mission? How would you react?

An Exercise

Here are some passages taken directly from the books of the prophets. Try to match them to the common characteristics of prophets stated above by placing the number of the characteristic next to the passage:

A. _____ God answered me and said, "Write the prophecy down and inscribe it clearly on tablets so that it can be read with clarity." (Habakkuk 2:2)

B. _____ "Hark!" one says, "Proclaim." And he says, "What shall I proclaim?" "All flesh is grass and all the good is as the flower of the field. The grass withers and the flowers fade when a wind of God blows on it. Surely the people are like grass. The grass withers and the flowers fade, but the word of our God will endure forever." (Isaiah 40:6–8)

C. _____ "Comfort, comfort you My people," says God. Speak tenderly to Jerusalem and declare to her that her term of service is over, and her iniquity is expiated. (Isaiah 40:1–2)

D. _____ Then I said: "But God, behold, I cannot speak. I am only a child." But God said to me, "Do not say 'I am a child' for to whomever I send you, you will go, and whatever I command, so you will say." (Jeremiah 1:6–7)

E. _____ The word of God thus came to me a second time: "Jeremiah, what do you see?" And I said, "I see a boiling pot which is facing north." And God said to me: "Out of the north evil will break forth upon all the inhabitants of the land." (Jeremiah 1:13–14)

F. _____ God said to me, "O mortal, stand on your feet so that I can speak to you." As God spoke to me, a spirit entered into me and set me upon my feet. God said to me, "O mortal, I am sending you to the people of Israel, that nation of rebels, who have rebelled against Me." (Ezekiel 2:1–3)

G. _____ Hear this, you who trample upon the needy and bring the poor of the land to the end saying, "When will the new moon be over, that we may sell grain? And [when will] the Sabbath [be over], that we may offer wheat for sale, that we may make the ephah small and the shekel great, and deal deceitfully with false balances? [When will the Sabbath be over so] that we may buy the poor for silver, and the needy for a pair of sandals, and sell the refuse of the wheat?" (Amos 8:4–6)

H. _____ Bringing oblations is futile, and incense is offensive to me. . . . Your new moon and fixed seasons fill Me with loathing. They have become a burden to Me. (Isaiah 1:13-14)

I. _____ Why must my pain be endless, my wound incurable, resistant to healing? You have been to me like a spring that fails, like waters that are unreliable. (Jeremiah 15:18)

J. _____ "Is it My desire that a wicked person dies?" says God. "It is rather that he [or she] turn back from his [or her] ways and live." (Ezekiel 18:23)

K. _____ God has shown you what is good and what is required of you: do justly, love kindness, and walk humbly with God. (Micah 6:8)

L. _____ The lion has roared; who will not fear? God has spoken; who can [do anything] but prophesy? (Amos 3:8)

M. _____ I saw this great vision, and I became powerless. My appearance was destroyed, and my strength deserted me. (Daniel 10:8)

N. _____ Woe is Me! I am undone. . . . For My eyes have seen the King. (Isaiah 6:5)

The Spectrum of Jewish Belief: Reform, Conservative, and All the Rest

As Reform Judaism evolved, it emphasized ethics over ritual. It stressed the "right" over the "rite." As a result, it championed a Judaism of ethical monotheism, and used the ancient Hebrew prophets as models. The social action program that identified the Reform movement during the 1950s, 1960s, and 1970s grew out of this fundamental commitment to a particular understanding of Hebrew prophecy. The social action agenda remains an important part of the Reform ideology, and it has been called by Rabbi Eric Yoffie the crown jewel in the Reform Jewish crown. While the Conservative movement did not see the necessary parallel between prophecy and social action, one seminal Conservative thinker, Rabbi Abraham Joshua Heschel, certainly did. When he marched for civil rights in the

South in the 1960s he did so as a response to the will of the Hebrew prophets. As would be expected, Orthodox Judaism accepts the ancient Hebrew prophets as they are described in the Bible and interpreted throughout rabbinic literature.

PRINCIPLE SEVEN

Moses, Our Teacher

I believe with perfect faith that the prophecy of Moses is absolutely true. He is the chief of all prophets, both those before and after him.

Getting Started: A Brief Introduction to Moses

The seventh principle of faith involves Moses, proclaiming his superiority to all other prophets, whether they preceded him or came afterwards. Before we can determine whether or not there are valid reasons for naming Moses the chief of the prophets, it would be wise to briefly present his biography, so that you can better become acquainted with the man who was a leader, prophet, and a lawgiver.

The primary sources for the story of Moses' life and works are contained in the books of Exodus, Leviticus, Numbers, and Deuteronomy. Additional references are found in other biblical books, including Joshua, Judges, the Books of Samuel and Kings, Isaiah, Hosea, Micah, Malachi, Psalms, Daniel, Nehemiah, and Chronicles.

Moses lived around the year 1300 B.C.E. His mother and father were Yocheved and Amram, both of the tribe of Levi. He had an older sister Miriam and an older brother Aaron. Moses was born at the height of the Egyptian persecution of Israel. The Pharaoh who "knew not Joseph" (Exodus 1:8) had set taskmasters over the children of Israel to oppress them with forced labor. In order to reduce their numbers, Pharaoh had also instructed the Hebrew midwives, Shiphrah and Puah, to kill the Israelite boys at birth. When the plan failed, Pharaoh directed all his people to throw every newborn Hebrew boy into the Nile River. Moses' mother, Yocheved, managed to conceal her baby for three months. Then, when she thought that she could conceal him no longer, she made a wicker basket for him and placed him among the reeds of the river, while his sister, Miriam, watched from a distance. Pharaoh's daughter, seeing the basket when she came down to bathe, ordered one of her maids to fetch it. The princess took pity on the crying infant, and decided to adopt him. At Miriam's own suggestion, Moses' own mother was given the task of nursing the child until he was old enough to be returned to Pharaoh's daughter. In this way, Moses the Hebrew was, ironically, brought up as a prince in Pharaoh's own palace.

We know very little about the early years of Moses. His first pursuit of justice as an adult ended in tragedy. It occurred when Moses saw an Egyptian beating a fellow Hebrew. Here is the biblical account:

> After Moses had grown up, he went out to his kinsfolk and witnessed their toil. He saw an Egyptian beating a Hebrew, one of his kinsmen. He looked around and upon seeing that no one was about, he struck down the Egyptian, and hid his body in the sand. When he went out the next day, he found two Hebrews fighting, so Moses said to the offender, "Why do you strike your fellow?" He retorted, "Who made you chief and ruler over us? Do you mean to kill me as you killed the Egyptian?" Moses was frightened, and thought (to himself): The matter must be known! When Pharaoh learned what had happened, he sought to kill Moses; but Moses fled from Pharaoh.
> (Exodus 2:11–15)

The lack of details in this Exodus text has left a lot of room for rabbis to "fill in the gaps." The Bible does not moralize and take a stand on Moses' act of violence. Nowhere is there an explicit evaluation that either praises or condemns it. The text does not reveal whether Moses killed the Egyptian deliberately or whether he beat him so severely that he died. You, the reader, are left to decide, and to make your own conclusions.

What do you think? Does this behavior early in Moses' career portray greatness, or do you believe that Moses shows a lack of self-discipline, which, is a requisite to true leadership?

Some rabbis believed that it was this act of manslaughter that kept Moses from entering the Promised Land. Others maintained that although Moses was a person of high ideals and great moral courage, at this point in his life he still lacked the self-discipline required for true leadership. In the commentary Me-Am Lo'ez, regarding the verse, "Moses saw an Egyptian beating a Hebrew," it says that "righteousness begins when one sees the yoke others bear."

Flight to Midian and the Mission

In Midian, once again Moses rose to defend the persecuted. He saved the daughters of Jethro the priest (his future father-in-law), who had come to water their father's flocks from the hands of the bullying local shepherds. As a result of the incident, Moses stayed with Jethro, and married his daughter Zipporah. They had two sons, Gershom and Eliezer. It was in the timeless desert, tending Jethro's flocks, that Moses slowly matured.

The Turning Point: The Call from God

The turning point in the career of Moses came when he got a glimpse of the Divine in the region of Horeb. Here are the biblical verses of this remarkable story:

> Now, Moses, tending the flock of his father-in-law, Jethro, the priest of Midian, drove the flock into the wilderness, and came to Horeb, the mountain of God. An angel of God appeared to him in a blazing fire out of a bush. Moses gazed, and there was a bush all aflame, yet the bush was not consumed. Moses said: "I must turn aside to look at this marvelous sight; why doesn't the bush burn up?" When God saw that he had turned aside to look, God called to him out of the bush: "Moses, Moses." And he answered: "*Heneini* [a phrase the Torah uses to announce that something significant is about to happen], or here I am." And God said, "Do not come closer.

Remove your sandals from your feet, for the place on which you stand is holy ground."

(Exodus 3:1–5)

What do you think convinced God to finally call Moses directly after the first appearance of the angel? Do you think that God saw any particular quality of leadership in Moses that convinced God to send Moses on his mission?

Hint: Some commentators have suggested that God may have been testing Moses' attention span, an important attribute of any prophet. What might have, as it were, convinced God that Moses was attentive was the ability of Moses to "hang around" long enough to realize that the bush that he envisioned as burning was "not being consumed." Think about it. There were lots of bushes in the desert, and apparently they burned frequently (the result of the hot desert sun blazing on the dry bushes).

Textual Encounters: Moses' Faith and His Excuses

Moses raises a series of objections to God before he accepts the mission, revealing a man who, not only feels unworthy of the task, but also had doubts about the efficacy of the mission itself. The following is a summary of his objections. After reading each of them, decide whether you feel that the objections are truly characteristic of a person who was well chosen to lead a primitive people out of their Egyptian bondage.

Objection 1

Moses feels inadequate to the task: After God has told Moses that he is the one who will be sent to Pharaoh to free the Israelites, Moses says, "Who am I that I should go to Pharaoh and free the Israelites from Egypt?" (Exodus 3:11)

Objection 2

Moses again feels inadequate to the task: Moses is told in Exodus 3:18 by God, "The people will listen to you." To this Moses demurs, and says, "What if they do not believe me, and do not listen to me?" (Exodus 4:1)

[Note: The commentator Rashi describes Moses as one who had little faith.]

Objection 3

Moses inquires into God's name: Moses concluded that God could best be approached and understood if he knew God's name. Moses therefore says to God, "When I come to the Israelites and say to them 'the God of your ancestors has sent me to you,' and they ask me, 'What is God's name?', what shall I say to them?" (Exodus 3:13–14)

Objection 4

Moses has a speech challenge: Moses says to God, "Please, O God, I have never been a man of words either in times past or now that You have spoken to Your servant. I am slow of speech and slow of tongue." (Exodus 4:10)

Objection 5

Moses refuses his mission with no argument. After Moses is told by God that God will be with him and will instruct him exactly as to what to say, Moses says, "Please, God, make someone else Your agent." (Exodus 4:13)

Patiently God answers each objection, stating that God will be with Moses. God tells Moses that the Israelites, following their departure from Egypt, will serve God at this mountain. That would be a sign to Moses that God had sent him. Moses was to tell the people that "I am that I am" had spoken to him, and that God, who gives humans speech, would teach them what to say. Together with the elders he was to ask Pharaoh's permission for the Israelites to go on a three-day journey into the wilderness to make sacrifices to God, although the request would certainly be refused (4:29–5:1). To help him convince the Israelites, God gave Moses three wondrous signs (the rod becomes a snake and is restored to its former state; Moses' hand becomes leprous and is healed; the Nile water, poured out on the ground, turns to blood—Exodus 4). But still, without further rational argument, Moses refuses. God is angered, but promises to let Aaron be Moses' spokesperson, and asks him to take the rod with which to perform these signs (Exodus 4:13–17; 7:1–2). With this assurance Moses appears ready to assume the responsibility of his mission.

Have there ever been times when you were about to take upon yourself a mission of responsibility and you found excuses for choosing not to take them on? In what way were your objections similar to those of Moses? Were you able to resolve your feelings and gain the necessary strength to carry out your task? If so, what was the turning point for you? Did it take someone to convince you that you would not fail in your task?

Leadership and Ultimate Responsibility

Good leadership demands total devotion. It is never automatic. When a person such as Moses was chosen to a position of leadership, he was forever bound to the Israelite community, with all of its burdens resting on him. Following are several biblical scenarios where Moses is put into a position where he must take immediate action. Your mission is to read each of these passages, and to decide whether you agree or disagree with the course of action that Moses chose to take. If you disagree, decide what action you would have taken had you been Moses. Do you think that Moses displayed actions that deemed him worthy of the title given him by Maimonides of "chief of the prophets?"

Moses the Legislator

It came to pass on the morrow, that Moses sat as magistrate among the people, while the people stood about Moses from morning until evening. But when Moses' father-in-law (Jethro) saw how much he had to do for the people, he said, "What is this thing that you have undertaken for the people? Why do you act alone, while all the people stand about you from morning until evening? Moses replied to his father-in law, "It is because the people come to me to inquire of God. When they have an argument, it comes to my attention, and I arbitrate between a person and a neighbor, and I make known the laws and teachings of God." (Exodus 18:13–16)

Do you agree with Moses' leadership style of taking time to listen to each and every dispute of the Israelites? If you do not agree, what advice would you give to him? Here is the advice that his father-in law Jethro gave to him. After reading it, decide on whether you would have offered similar advice.

Moses' father-in-law said to him, "The thing you are doing is not right, you will surely wear yourself out, you as well as this people. The task is too burdensome for you. You cannot do it yourself. Now listen to me, I will give you counsel, and may God be with you. . . . You shall seek out from among the people capable individuals who fear God, trustworthy people who spurn ill-gotten gains. And set these over them as chiefs . . . Let them exercise authority over the people at all times. Let them bring every major dispute to you, but decide every minor dispute themselves. Make it easier for yourself, and let them share the burden with you." (Exodus 18:17, 21–22)

Moses accepts his father-in-law's advice. Do you think that he should have accepted it? What do you think of Jethro's system of legislation? How does one decide which case is important and which is only a so-called "minor" one? Do you feel that Moses is really the top of the leadership cadre, or is the top really God?

Who is Responsible: The Story of the Golden Calf

When the people saw that Moses took so long to come down from the mountain, they gathered against Aaron and said to him, "Come, make us a god who shall go before us, for that man Moses, who brought us from the land of Egypt—we cannot tell what has happened to him." Aaron said to them, "Take off the gold rings that are on the ears of your wives, your sons, and your daughters, and bring them to me." And all the people took off the gold rings that were in their ears and brought them to Aaron. . . . Then God spoke to Moses, "Hurry down, for your people whom you brought from the land of Egypt have acted badly." . . . God further said to Moses, "I see that this is a stiff necked people. Now let Me be, so that My anger may blaze forth against them, so that I may destroy them, and make of you a great nation." But Moses implored God, "Do not let your anger, O God, blaze forth against Your people, whom You delivered from the land of Egypt. . . . Do not let the Egyptians say, 'It is with evil intent that God delivered them, only to kill them off in the mountains and annihilate them from the face of the earth.' Turn from Your blazing anger, and renounce the plan to punish Your people. Remember your servants Abraham, Isaac and Jacob, how You swore to them Yourself and said to them: 'I will make your offspring as numerous as the stars of the heaven, and I will give to your offspring this whole land of which I spoke, to possess forever.'" So God renounced the punishment which God had planned to bring to the people.

(Exodus 32:1–3, 4, 7–14)

What do you think of the leadership style of Moses in his interaction with God? Would you have used similar arguments? Why do you think that Moses' arguments were able to change God's mind? Have you ever been in a situation where someone was about to be punished and you were able to persuade someone to change the punishment he or she had in mind? How were you able to do it?

The text now continues, and as Moses approaches the camp of the Israelites, this is what he sees and how he reacts:

As soon as Moses came near the camp and saw the calf and the dancing, he became enraged. He hurled the tablets from his hands and shattered them at the foot of the mountain. He took the calf that they had made and burnt it; he ground it to powder and strewed it upon the water and made the Israelites drink it. . . .

Moses saw that the people were out of control, since Aaron had let them get out of control, so that they were a menace to any who might oppose them. Moses then stood up in the gate of the camp and said, "Whoever is for God, come here." And all the Levites rallied to him. He said to them, "Thus says God, the God of Israel. Each of you put your sword on your hip, go back and forth from gate to gate throughout the camp, and slay brother, neighbor, and kin. The Levites did as Moses had bidden, and some three thousand of the people fell that day. . . . The next day Moses said to the people, "You have been guilty of a great sin. Yet I will now go up to God. Perhaps I may win forgiveness for your sin." Moses went back to God and said, "Alas this people is guilty of a great sin in making for themselves a god of gold. And yet, if You would only forgive them their sin. If not, erase me from the record which You have written." God said to Moses, "The one who has sinned against Me will I erase from My record. . . ."

(Exodus 32:19–20, 25–28, 30–33)

What is your reaction to Moses hurling the holy tablets to the ground when he saw the dancing around the calf? Should Moses have been better able to control his anger? What do you think you would have done if you were Moses?

What is your reaction to the slaying of the three thousand Israelites by the Levites? Was this a fair punishment to be imposed by Moses? What was Moses trying to accomplish?

Finally, what is your reaction to Moses' strategy when asking God to forgive the people of Israel?

Moses as Intercessor

The stories of Israel's trials of God during their journey fall into two groups: the pre-Sinai trials, in which God's saving power is shown after Moses cries to God (as seen in the Golden Calf story), and the post-Sinai trials, in which the Israelites are punished for their faithlessness. Moses is constantly called upon to intercede on their behalf to assuage God's anger. In the following excerpt from the text, Moses is angry over Israel's disbelief in his capacity to give them victory over the Canaanites. Once again, God threatens to destroy Israel, and, once again, Moses intercedes on the people's behalf. Here is the story in the Torah's words:

The Israelites cried and said, "If only we had meat to eat. We remember the fish that we used to eat free in Egypt." ... Moses heard the weeping, group after group, every person at the entrance of his tent. God was very angry, and Moses was very distressed. Moses said to God, "Why have you dealt ill with Your servant, and why have I not enjoyed your favor, that You have laid the burden of all this people upon me.... I cannot carry all this people by myself, for it is too much for me. If You would deal thus with me, kill me rather, I beg You, and let me see no more of my wretchedness...."
(Numbers 11:4–5,10–11, 13–15)

The whole community broke into loud cries, and the people wept that night. All the Israelites railed against Moses and Aaron. "If only we had died in the land of Egypt...."

And God said to Moses, "How long will this people spurn Me, and how long will they have no faith in Me despite all the signs that I have performed in their midst? I will strike them with pestilence and disown them.".... Then Moses replied to God,] "If you slay this people, the nations who have heard Your fame will say, 'it must be because God was powerless to bring that people into the land which God had promised.'... Therefore, please let my God's forbearance be great, as You have declared, saying, 'God, slow to anger and abounding in kindness.'... Please pardon the sin of this people according to Your great kindness.".... So God said, "I pardon, as you have asked...."
(Numbers 14:1–2, 11–12, 15-20)

How would you rate Moses as an advocate for his people? In what ways were his arguments to God compelling? In what ways might you make use of Moses' arguments when you need to intercede on behalf of someone else? Think of a time when you needed to help someone who was about to be punished. What did you do to show your persuasive leadership ability?

The Striking of the Rock

The desert wanderings were, for understandable reasons, a period of constant tension and crisis. The people lacked food, and were not content with the heavenly manna. At times they demanded meat, and they were often in need of drinking water. Like many of us, they constantly complained. Nothing was ever good enough. Following is the text related to the famous incident of Moses striking the rock:

> And there was no water for the congregation, and they assembled themselves together against Moses and against Aaron. And the people strove with Moses and spoke saying: "Would that we had died when our brethren died before God. . . . Why did you bring us out of Egypt, to bring us to this evil place? It is no place of seed, or of figs, or of vines, or of pomegranates; neither is there any water.". . . God replied to Moses, "Take the rod and assemble the congregation and you and Aaron your brother. Speak to the rock before their eyes, that it may give forth its water so that you shall give the people and their cattle drink." Moses took the rod from before God, as God instructed him. And Moses and Aaron gathered the assembly together before the rock, and said to them: "Hear now you rebels, are we to bring you forth water out of this rock?" And Moses lifted up his hand and smote the rock with his rod twice; and water gushed forth and the people drank, and their cattle too. And God said: "Because you did not believe in Me, to sanctify Me in the eyes of the Israelites, you shall not bring this assembly into the land which I have given them."
> (Numbers 20:2–5, 7–12)

Moses was told to speak to the rock, and instead, he struck it twice with his rod. According to the traditional interpretation of this event, Moses was prohibited from entering the Promised Land. In your opinion, do you feel that his punishment fits the crime? What specifically was the offense of Moses? Why was God was offended? Could there have been another reason that Moses was prevented from entering the Promised Land?

Biblical Summary of Moses' Unique Status

In the Book of Deuteronomy (34:10), the unique status of Moses is summarized: "There has not risen a prophet since in Israel like Moses, whom God knew face to face." This verse likely influenced Maimonides' belief in the preeminence of Moses, so much so that Maimonides included Moses in one of the articles of Maimonides' creed. Here is a summary of other biblical references which clearly point to the unique status of Moses as a prophet and teacher.

1. The wonders performed by Moses on behalf of Israel exceeded those of any subsequent prophet. (Deuteronomy 34:11–12)

2. He outdid all of Egypt's magicians. (Exodus 7:8–13)

3. He prevailed against the mightiest forces of nature, splitting both the Sea of Reeds (Exodus 14:15–25) and the earth. (Numbers 16:28–33)

4. He was able to endure, on more than one occasion, a fast of forty days. (Deuteronomy 9:9, 19)

5. Moses is portrayed as speaking to God "face to face" (Exodus 33:11), allowing him to share an unparalleled intimacy with God.

6. Moses' face was so radiant with God's Presence that at one point, he had to wear a veil in his ordinary interaction with people. (Exodus 34:30–35)

7. While God spoke to other prophets in dreamlike visions, God spoke with Moses "mouth to mouth." (Numbers 12:8)

8. Moses is called a "man of God." (Deuteronomy 33:1)

Rabbinic Views of Moses

A marked ambivalence can be observed in rabbinic tradition toward the personality of Moses. On the one hand, Moses is the greatest of all the Jewish teachers. Unlike other prophets, Moses is known in Jewish tradition as *Moshe Rabbenu* (Moses Our Teacher), not Moses the Prophet or Moses the Leader.

There appears to be a constant attempt to affirm the supremacy of Moses while, at the same time, carefully denying him any divine honors.

In speaking about Moses, Rav and Mar Samuel said that he had "fifty gates of understanding, [and he was] a littler lower than the angels" (Talmud, Nedarim 38a). All the prophets saw God as one looks into a dim glass, but Moses was one who looks through a clear glass (Talmud, Yevamot 49b). When Moses was born the whole house was filled with light (Talmud, Sotah 12a). Moses was so kind, gentle and considerate to his sheep when tending the flock of Jethro his father-in-law that God made him the shepherd of Israel (Exodus Rabbah 2:2). It was Rabbi Yochanan who said: "The Holy Blessed One causes Divine Presence to rest only upon one who is strong, wealthy, wise and humble and Moses had all of these qualifications" (Talmud, Nedarim 38a).

According to one rabbinic opinion, Moses did not really die but still stands and minsters to God as he did while on Mount Sinai (Talmud, Sotah 13b). Moses was righteous from the beginning of his life to the end of it (Talmud, Megillah 11a). The humility of Moses (and also Aaron) was greater than that of Abraham since Abraham spoke of himself as dust and ashes (Genesis 18:27), but Moses and Aaron declared that they were nothing at all (Exodus Rabbah 3:16). According to the talmudic tractate of Hullin 89a, the whole world existed only on account of the merit of Moses (and Aaron).

These and similar sayings are typical of the rabbinic determination to go to the utmost lengths in praising Moses.

As we have noted, the rabbis called Moses "Moses our Teacher" (*Moshe Rabbenu*). Yet there is no mention of this term in the Mishnah. Some scholars have suggested that the absence of the term in the Mishnah was a conscious anti-Christian reaction to the honor given to Jesus. Thus, to avoid any misunderstanding, they wanted to downplay the character of Moses. (See John 3:2.)

The Mishnah did not only heap praise on Moses. At times, the rabbis criticized him for things such as his quick temper (Talmud, Pesachim 66b, Sotah 13b). Sometimes, this was a balance to their criticism, noting, for example, that he erred. However, the rabbis quickly conceded that he acknowledged his mistake (Talmud, Zevachim 101a).

According to rabbinic tradition, Moses was given the Oral Law (*Torah she-be-al peh*) along with the Written Law (*Torah she-bikhtav*). This was one of the new ideas that the rabbis brought to the Jewish community while the priests still governed the community. According to the Jerusalem Talmud, whatever new interpretation of the law is ever brought before a teacher by a keen student of the Torah was already given to Moses at Mount Sinai (Peah 2:6, 17a). The innovative idea that new teachings were truly new and yet were implied in the Torah given to Moses is conveyed in a story about Moses traveling to the academy of Rabbi Akiva. Moses was disturbed that he was unable to comprehend Akiva's teachings. Then, Akiva really unnerved Moses when he declared that he had received the teaching as a tradition from Moses at Sinai (Talmud, Menachot 29b). The idea that the foremost Jewish teachers who produced innovations, such as Hillel, Yochanan ben Zakkai, and Akiva, are identified with Moses, whose work they continued, is expressed in the statement that they, like Moses, also lived for 120 years. The rabbis explain that each lived a period of forty years (Sifrei, Deuteronomy 327).

The rabbis also praised Moses for his honesty. Accordingly, when Moses announced the final plague against the Egyptians, the slaying of the firstborn, he did not state the exact time it was initiated. Moses only said that it would occur "about midnight" (Exodus 11:4), because he was afraid that Pharaoh's astrologers might miscalculate the time and declare him a liar (Talmud, Berachot 4a).

There are also numerous Moses stories in rabbinic tradition that reported his relationship with the angels of God. In one story (Talmud, Yoma 4a), Moses went up to Sinai enveloped by a cloud which sanctified him for receiving the Torah. After Moses ascended on high, the ministering angels contested the right of "one born of woman to receive the treasures of the Torah." Encouraged by God, Moses demonstrated to the angels that only humans were subject to the Torah's regulations, and therefore it was rightfully theirs. As a result, the angels became friendly with Moses, and each of them revealed its secrets to him (Talmud, Shabbat 89a).

The rabbis even try to explain away Moses' hesitation in accepting his mission (at the beginning of the Book of Exodus). They argued, for example, that Moses recoiled from the task, because of the honor and prestige that would accrue to him for successfully completing it (Tanchuma, Leviticus 3). On another occasion, they explained that Moses was afraid that in accepting the mission he would be trespassing upon his older brother's domain whom Moses felt should be the redeemer. (Exodus Rabbah 3:16). Finally, the rabbis suggested that Moses wanted God to redeem the Israelites, rather than he, a human, because he felt that a Divine redemption would be eternal (Exodus Rabbah 3:4). All of these rabbinic explanations attempt to explain away anything that might detract from Moses' character.

According to one rabbinic tradition, Moses died at the kiss of God (Deuteronomy Rabbah 11:10) on his birthday, Adar 7. Then God buried Moses (Talmud, Sotah 14a) in a grave that the Holy One had prepared for him on the eve of the Sabbath of creation.

Maimonides on Moses

According to Maimonides' seventh principle, Moses was chief of all the prophets and superior to all of them. In his writings, Maimonides presented four of his distinguishing features:

1. God spoke to all prophets through an intermediary, but Moses did not need one. How do we know? "Mouth to mouth I will speak to him." (Numbers 12:8)

2. Every other prophet could receive prophecy only while sleeping. To Moses, however, the word came by day, when Moses stood fully awake

before the two cherubim. God thus testified: "I will meet you with you there, and I will speak with you from above the ark cover, from between the two cherubim that are on the ark of testimony." (Exodus 25:22)

3. Prophets experienced visions that were traumatic for them, weakening them. For instance, after the angel Gabriel spoke to Daniel in a vision, Daniel said, "I became powerless, my appearance was disarrayed" (Daniel 10:8). However, this was not true of Moses. The word came to him and he did not experience terror or exhaustion. Thus the Torah says that God spoke to Moses "face to face, as a person speaks to a friend." (Exodus 33:11)

4. Other prophets could not receive prophecy whenever they desired. It all depended on God's will, and they often had to wait days or even years to receive prophecy. Moses, on the other hand, could achieve prophecy whenever he desired, that is, he could enter into dialogue with God whenever he wanted to do so.

Maimonides called Moses the greatest prophet, and included his prophecy in his principles of faith, because of what happened at Mount Sinai, witnessed by 600,000 (according to tradition). "Our eyes saw and not a stranger's. Our ears heard and not another's. The Voice of God spoke to him, and God spoke to Moses face-to-face." Thus, those who received Moses' message, that is, the people of Israel, became witnesses to his status as prophet. This was not the case with any other prophet.

One can summarize the importance of belief in Moses as the greatest prophet in the following statement in Maimonides' *Mishneh Torah*, specifically in the section called *Hilkhot Teshuvah*, Laws of Repentance: "In the category of the heretic, there are three different types of individuals [including] . . . one who denies the prophecy of Moses."

Personalizing the Principle of Faith

It is now your turn to try to formulate your own personal beliefs related to Moses and his greatness as prophet. Use these questions as guidelines.

I. Do you believe that Moses was the greatest prophet who ever lived? What are your reasons for this belief? (Note: If you do not believe that Moses was the greatest of all prophets, then who do you choose, and why?)

2. In what ways to do you think that Moses differed from other prophets?

3. According to an old Jewish tradition, we call Moses *Moshe Rabbenu*/Moses our teacher. Do you think that this is a proper way to describe him? What has Moses taught the Jewish people? (Note: If you do not think that Moshe Rabbenu is the best term to describe Moses, what term do you feel is most appropriate for him? Perhaps it should be Moses the Leader, Moses the Prophet, Moses the Intercessor, etc.)

4. Simeon Ben Zoma, a rabbi who lived almost nineteen centuries ago, once asked: "Who is a strong leader?" His answer: The one who conquers one's passions and emotions. (Pirke Avot 4:I.) How do you think Ben Zoma would rate the quality of Moses' leadership?

5. Rabbi Judah Nesiah and the rabbis disagreed. One said, "According to the leader, so goes the generation." The other said, "According to the generation, so goes the leader" (Talmud, Arachin 17a). Which statement do you feel better reflects the history of Moses and the Israelites of his time?

6. Rabbi Nachman of Bratzlav one said: When a person is able to take abuse with a smile, that person is worthy of becoming a leader. How do you think Rabbi Nachman of Bratzlav would rate Moses as a leader?

7. What is the most important thing that Moses has taught you?

8. Why, according to Maimonides, do you think that it is important that Moses is rendered the greatest of all the prophets? Why do you think that Moses had to be rated with such a high level of prophecy?

9. What do you believe is Moses' greatest strength? What is his greatest weakness?

10. It is of interest to note that Moses is mentioned more than any other biblical figure in the New Testament. Why do you think this is the case?

11. Why do you believe Moses was ultimately denied entry into the Promised Land?

12. If prophecy involves the understanding of important universal truths, then it should be available to the people of every nation. In your opinion, do the people of other religions also have legitimate claims to prophetic illumination?

One Final Question

What did you learn about Moses that will have lasting impact on your life?

PRINCIPLE EIGHT

The Light of Torah

I believe with perfect faith that the whole Torah, now in our possession, is the same one that was given to Moses our teacher, peace be to him.

Getting Started: Some Background

Traditional Jews believe that the Torah as we know it was given by God on Mount Sinai, where it was written down. Moses taught the Jewish people about God through the Torah. According to rabbinic tradition, God also used the Torah as a blueprint for creating the world. Moreover, the Torah is a record of the evolving relationship between the Jewish people and God. So, says the tradition, it is without error. The entire structure of the Torah provides meaning for our lives. Each word—even the spaces between the words—offers us nearly unlimited insight into God and our relationship with the divine.

Nontraditional Jews may differ among themselves about the origin of the Torah, but they all agree that it was not given on Mount Sinai by God to Moses in its present form. Rabbi Isaac Mayer Wise, the organizing founder of American Reform Judaism, believed that most of the Torah was written by humans, but that the Ten Commandments were given word for word as we have them by God. (With this approach, he affirmed their name in Hebrew: *Aseret ha-Dibrot*—literally, the Ten Utterances.) Liberal Jews will argue that the Torah is made up of numerous documents. (This argument is generally referred to as the Documentary Hypothesis, a theory that developed in Germany in the nineteenth century.) That accounts for its many apparent internal contradictions. Take a look at the two apparently different stories of human creation in the early chapters of Genesis. Pay special attention to the way in which man and woman were created in each story and other instructions that God gave them. Notice too, that in Text 1 the Hebrew word used for God is the generic Elohim, while in Text 2 the Hebrew word for God is YHVH (pronounced Adonai) and Elohim.

Text 1: Genesis 1:26–30

God said: "Let us make the human in our image, after our likeness, and let them have dominion over the fish of the sea, and over the fowl of the air, and over the cattle, and over all the earth, and over every creeping thing that creeps on the earth." So God created the human in the Divine image, in the image of God, created God them. God blessed them and said to them: "Be fruitful and multiply. Replenish the earth and subdue it. Take dominion over the fish of the sea, over the fowl of the air, and over every living thing that creeps on the earth." Then God said: "Behold, I have given you every herb yielding seed which is on the face of all the earth, and every tree, in which is the fruit of a tree yielding seed—to you it shall be for food. And to every beast of the earth, to every fowl of the air and to everything that creeps on the earth, where there is a living soul, I have given every green here for food." And it was so.

Text 2: Genesis 2:7–9, 15–24

Then Adonai Elohim formed the human out of the dust of the ground, and breathed into his nostrils the breath of life. And the human became a living soul. So Adonai Elohim planted a garden eastward in Eden, and there put the human whom Adonai Elohim had formed. Adonai Elohim made to grow out of the ground every tree that is pleasant to the sight and good for food. (Adonai Elohim also placed) the tree of life in the midst of the garden, as well as the tree of knowledge of good and evil.... Then Adonai Elohim took the human, and placed the human in the garden of Eden to tend to it.... Next Adonai Elohim said, "It is not good for the human to be alone; I will make a companion for him." ... The human gave names to the cattle and the fowl of the air, and name every beast in the field. But there remained no (human) companion for him. So Adonai Elohim caused a deep sleep to fall upon the human. While he slept, Adonai Elohim took one of his ribs, and closed up the place with flesh instead. With the rib which Adonai Elohim had taken from the human, Adonai Elohim made a woman and brought her to the man. And the man said, "This is now bone of my bones, flesh of my flesh. She shall be called woman, because she was taken out of man. Therefore shall a man leave his father and his mother and shall cleave unto his wife, and they shall become one flesh.

Editors who represent a certain point of view shaped the text so it would reflect what they most wanted the reader to get out of it. The Torah is the God-inspired work of humans, the result of revelation as interpreted by the "religious geniuses" of the day as philosopher and theologian Rabbi Eugene B. Borowitz likes to call the authors of the Torah. Through the course of history, as the Torah was transmitted from one generation to the next, various editors continued to shape the Torah. Of course, they edited the text in a way to make their viewpoint dominant (so the priestly editors, as they were called, emphasized the centrality of the Temple cult and the role of the priests).

The flood story is a combination of the source called J, in which God is called Jehovah, according to German Christian scholars, or what we refer to as Adonai, and the P, or Priestly School, named for the priests who role figures prominantly in ancient Israel. The following excerpt contains verses from the Flood story with those identified from the P source in bold print. After you have read the story, list the differences between the two versions.

Genesis 6

5) Adonai saw that the evil of humans was great on the earth, and all the inclination of the thoughts of their heart was only evil all day.

6) Adonai regretted having made humans in the earth, and Adonai grieved in His heart.

12) God saw that the earth was corrupted, for all flesh had corrupted its way on the earth.

13) Of all the living, of all flesh, you shall bring two to the ark to keep alive with you; they shall be male and female.

Genesis 7:

2) Of all the clean beasts, take yourself seven pairs, male and female; and of the beasts which are not clean, two, male and female.

3) Also of the birds of the heavens seven pairs, male and female, to keep alive seed on the face of the earth.

8) Of the clean beasts and of the beasts which were not clean, and of the birds and all of those which creep upon the earth.

9) Two of each came to Noah to the ark, male and female, as God had instructed Noah.

Genesis 8:

7) And he sent out a raven, and it went back and forth until the waters dried up from the earth.

8) And he sent out a dove from him to see whether the waters had eased from the face of the earth.

What details of the story are different in each of the versions? In which version does God show more feeling for the living creatures which God created?

Unfortunately, too many people focus on the documentary (sources) aspect of the discussion of Torah. By rejecting the divine authorship of the Torah, they often dismiss the teachings of the Torah itself, as well. Such people assume that the editors were primitive and thus did not realize that they were giving us a text that contained some contradictions and some redundancy. They quickly wrote them off as naive and unsophisticated. However, we believe that the editors knew precisely what they were doing. Because we live in the late twentieth century, we may have a different way of looking at sacred literature. Nevertheless, it is our job to figure out what these ancient editors were trying to teach us. Critics preoccupy themselves with the specific origin of the text while forgetting the most important thing: Torah was a result of the revelation of God to the Jewish people at a mountain we call Sinai. Regardless of the specificity of the details, we believe that revelation did take place. The sacred text that "recorded" that revelation has been handed down to us pretty much in the form we have to come to know. Thus, our obligation is not to argue about the specific details of its origin. Rather, we have to try to understand the Torah's message for our lives, regardless of the road the sacred text traveled throughout Jewish history. We do not study the Torah in order to learn more about the text. Instead, we study the Torah in order to learn more about ourselves. We can make the lives we live become the sacred texts. By what we do, we have the obligation to become Torah.

How Do We Make Ourselves Torah?

The revelation of Torah did not begin and end at Sinai. The revelation of God to the Jewish people continues to this day. We merely have to be open to the experience of it. Often there is too much noise in the world to hear God speaking to us. Perhaps what we need is what Rabbi Lawrence Kushner likes to call a spiritual Dolby noise-reduction system. This will help us tune out unnecessary noise (interference) and leave us only with the clear melody of Torah. We hear the reverberations and echoes of Torah in other sacred literature. That is why we often use the word Torah to refer to all Jewish sacred texts, as well as the insights that teachers have garnered through their study and offered to us.

For Maimonides, this principle of faith (no. 8) refers to Torah as both a written law, the law that Moses received and wrote down, and an oral law, the Torah that Moses received and passed down orally through the generations before it was eventually written down for us (what is generally called the Talmud). As we have learned in the previous chapter, this notion of an oral law is what made the rabbinic leadership different from the priests who preceded them. Some even argue that the rabbis used the notion of an oral law—as well as some other issues like reward and punishment in an afterlife and resurrection of the dead—to wrestle communal authority away from the priests.

For us, Torah is a dynamic principle—one that best describes our ongoing attempt to understand God's direction for our lives through our interaction with sacred text. But in order to ascertain God's guidance, we have to be willing to immerse ourselves in the Torah text through study and reflection. We have to enter the lives of the biblical characters and live with them. We have to become one with the text. This may seem like a difficult or even impossible process. As a result you may not be willing to try. Take it from us. It is well worth it. By engaging in Torah study, you can reach beyond yourself, into the heavens. In order to do so, we have to struggle with the crises of faith of all those ancestors we meet in the Bible, and make them our own—even as they reflect many of our own concerns. And as we leave those who came before us behind in the text, we find that they have changed us and we, in our understanding of them, have changed them as well. We have left a little of ourselves in the Torah. Our record of struggle has become part of the Torah.

Consider for a moment how you treat something precious to you, like a favorite stuffed animal or a baseball card. How about a love letter? Do you read it over and over? Do you study its contents looking for meaning in each and every word. Do you consider how the writer has inscribed his or her name and written a personal message to you? Even the placement of the stamp on the envelope provides us with something on which to reflect. And where do you keep this letter? Do you do your best to protect it from damage or from getting lost? And how do you preserve the letter so that you might share it with others many years—or many generations—from now?

The Torah is God's love letter to the Jewish people. We pore over its parchment scroll. We look for meaning in its words, in the way the letters are shaped and formed. We look at the vocabulary chosen and consider how God's name—the writer of the letter—is expressed. We have even devised a special ceremony that we use only when we read this "love letter" in public (*hakafot*, or Torah circuits). Even the communal reading of the Torah attempts to reenact or simulate the reception of the "love letter" as it was given to us (revelation at Sinai).

An Exercise

With the help of your rabbi, take the Torah out of the ark (*aron hakodesh*), and place it on the reading table (*bima*). Pay attention to all of its details. Make a list of everything you see, feel, smell—anything that impacts on your senses and emotions. Then turn it into a checklist for other Torah scrolls. For example, consider the way the scribe penned each letter. Compare this Torah to a second one, if possible. Note that each "love letter" is written just a little differently.

During the next public reading of the Torah, make mental notes of what is taking place. What are the elements of the service that make you feel like you are standing at Sinai awaiting revelation? How do you feel when the Torah is being read? Do you feel as though you were among the ancient Israelites, and Moses is reading the Torah to you? Later, when you are able, write down your thoughts, and bring them into class for you to review with others. Try to attend the same service with others in your class so that you can compare the experience. If you are able to attend services at other congregations, compare the way the Torah service is handled in different communities.

If you feel like the Torah service does not speak to you at all, make a list of things that could be done in the Torah reading that would help engage you as a congregant.

What about the Haftarah? Many people believe that the Haftarah was introduced into the worship service as a guise to fool vigilant authorities. The Seleucid ruler, Antiochus IV Epiphanes of Syria, forbade the study of Torah after his conquest of Jerusalem in 168 B.C.E. He thought that it perpetuated Jewish values and Judaism, which his rapacious program of Hellenizing sought to destroy. However, we believe that it was an effort by the rabbis to introduce more study into the service, particularly of those books that are read less frequently. Why do you think that we read the Haftarah—and only on Shabbat, holidays, and fasts? Consider how the Haftarah reading is handled in your synagogue. What suggestions do you have to make the reading (or its presentation) more engaging?

What We Believe

Now, let's unpack Maimonides' statement, trying to ascertain what he meant before we determine what this statement of religious belief means to us in our times.

I Believe

This is a personal statement of faith. Maimonides knew that he could not convince others about Jewish faith without probing it on his own. Another philosopher, Martin Buber, framed the same proposition a different way. He suggested that there are two aspects to our faith: one is inherited; the other is reasoned. We come to it on our own, based on our experiences in life, our encounters with the divine. In order to develop a strong religious belief that can carry us through life, we must grab hold of both perspectives. Accepting faith from one's parents (ancestors) may be a good place to begin, but we must also come to religious belief on our own terms.

Sometimes we say "I believe" in order to express our personal belief about something without imposing it on others. We can let others say what they feel; we do not have to speak for them. However, we have to acknowledge our role as models for other people, particularly those who may look up to us. Thus, their beliefs are informed by our own. That is why it is important to understand what Maimonides, perhaps the greatest Jewish philosopher of all time, believed.

Consider first the structure of religious belief that you have inherited. Which member of your family influences your religious beliefs more than anyone else? It may be a parent or grandparent, but it could also be a brother or sister, or even a cousin. What are the basic tenets of his or her belief? How did he or she come to them? How have they shared these beliefs with you? Do they express their beliefs in formal or informal contexts? How do you know what they believe? If you have not had a chance to discuss this with them in the past, take this opportunity to do so.

An Exercise

Using the statement "I believe," make a list of those things that you believe about the Torah. You may want to invite members of your family to contribute to this list, as well. Discuss the items on this list with one another, and see whether you agree or disagree. Make room for other opinions in your discussion.

A Ready Reference

Take a look in Exodus at Moses' receiving of the Torah on Mount Sinai. He prepared for the trek up the mountain, and instructed the people to prepare themselves, as well. However, the people grew restless during the forty days that Moses was up on the mountain. They were afraid that Moses had taken them out of Egypt, led them into the desert, and then, abandoned them. So they built a calf out of the golden jewelry that they had plundered from Egypt. When Moses saw what the people had done, he shattered the tablets he carried. Eventually, he ascended the mountain once again in order to receive a second set of tablets. (The tradition says that though these tablets were heavy, Moses did not carry them. Instead, the tablets carried Moses. The same thing was said of the ark of the covenant which the Israelites carried with them during their journey in the desert.) But what happened to this first set? According to rabbinic tradition, these broken tablets were placed alongside the whole ones in the portable ark which the Israelites carried as they made their way through the desert on the way to the Promised Land.

"With Perfect Faith"

As we have already learned, faith in Judaism is a constant struggle. It sounds like an oxymoron, but perfect faith in Judaism includes various imperfections. How do we have perfect faith in a document that we are trying to understand—that we do not understand fully, even if we believe that it was given or inspired by God?

"That the Torah now in our possession"
What are the obligations we have as inheritors of this Torah?

"Is the same that was given to Moses our teacher, peace be to him":

Moses is considered to be the greatest teacher in Jewish history, because he led us through the desert, and was instrumental in giving the Torah to the Jewish people. Many rabbis call Moses a prophet (because he was God's spokesperson). What do you think Moses did to warrant being called the greatest teacher?

Extending the Principle of Faith

Why do Jewish people study Torah? While some synagogues complete the reading of the Torah each year, others use a triennial cycle of reading. Some synagogues read the entire portion during Shabbat morning services, while others break up the reading on Mondays, Thursdays, and Saturdays. And some congregations select a portion of the Torah for public reading, that either has particular meaning for them or is a section that will be used for a *devar Torah*, or sermon. Regardless of the method chosen, we symbolically conclude our reading on Simchat Torah, and begin once again. (*Parashat Zot ha-Beracha* is reserved for this day and is not read on Shabbat.) When we read the Torah aloud in public assembly, we are attempting to reenact the revelation at Mount Sinai. Whenever we get a chance, we want to return to that time in the desert once again. It is one of the reasons that the Torah service concludes with a selection of sacred text: "Renew our days as of old" (Lamentations 5:21). In other words, we ask God, "Bring us back to the time of our desert journey when You, God, revealed yourself to us."

So, we study Torah to maintain that relationship that was initiated in the desert. In a metaphysical sense, we were all there—according to the Torah.

Personalizing the Principle of Faith

What relevance does it have to our lives, particularly as we face the challenges of our adolescence? How do I go about including Torah study in my life once I have determined that it has relevance? Torah has a place in your life. And so does God. The challenge you have is how to allow the voice of Torah to speak to you in words that you can understand, particularly as you are confronted by the rights and responsibilities of maturity. For example, how does admitting the Torah into one's life affect sexual decision-making and other issues of the body?

Textual Encounters

The Jewish people have been called the People of the Book. Study, learning, and a thirst for knowledge have always been important Jewish values. The knowledge of Torah was prized above worldly goods. The most honored figure in the life and culture of the traditional Jewish community was the *talmid chakham*, the wise student or scholar. Here are several texts, each dealing with a different aspect of Torah study. After reading each, answer the questions that follow.

Text I: Torah in the Face of Fear

Once the wicked Roman government issued a decree forbidding the Jews to study and practice Torah. Pappus ben Judah came by, and upon finding Rabbi Akiva publicly holding sessions in which he occupied himself with Torah, Pappus asked him: "Akiva, aren't you afraid of the government?" Akiva answered: "You, Pappus, who people say are wise, are, in fact, a fool." Let me explain what I mean by this parable:

A fox was walking on a river bank and seeing fishes swimming back and forth, asked them, "From whom are you fleeing?" They replied, "From the nets and traps set for us by humans." So the fox said to them, "How would you like to come up on dry land, so that you and I may live together the way my ancestors lived with yours?" They replied, "You, the cleverest of animals, are, in fact, a fool. If we are afraid of living in the place where we can stay alive, how much more afraid should we be in a place where we are sure to die."

So it is with us. If we are fearful when we sit and study Torah, of which it is written, "For it is your life and the length of your days" (Deuteronomy 30:20), how much more fearful should we be if we cease the study of words of Torah?

Soon after the encounter, Akiva was arrested and thrown into prison. Pappus ben Judah was also arrested, and put in jail next to Akiva. Rabbi Akiva asked, "Pappus, who brought you here?" He replied, "Happy are you, Rabbi Akiva, for you were seized for occupying yourself with Torah. Alas for Pappus who has been seized for occupying himself with vain things."

(Talmud, Berakhot 61b)

According to the Talmud, Rabbi Akiva was executed shortly after the conversation he had with Pappus. He died while saying the words of the *Shema*.

Questions:

What is the parable which is contained in this Talmudic story trying to teach? Why was Pappus arrested? What did Rabbi Akiva mean when he said, "How much more fearful should we be if we cease the study of words of Torah?" Given the ending of Akiva's life, what do you think it means in the *Shema*, in the paragraph often referred to as the *V'ahavta*, "To love God with all of your heart, soul, and might"? How is the study of Torah connected to the love of God?

Text 2: Torah is the Fountain of Life

a. Rabbi Judah said, in the name of Samuel, "What is meant by 'You make people as the fish of the sea' (Habakkuk 1:14)? In what way can humans be spoken of as being like the fish of the sea? In the case of the fish of the sea, once they go up on dry land, they promptly die. Also with human beings. As soon as they give up Torah and its precepts, they promptly perish."

(Talmud, Avodah Zarah 3a)

b. Words of Torah are compared to waters: "Everyone that is thirsty, come to the waters" (Isaiah 55:1). As waters reach from one end of the world to the other, so too does Torah reach from one end of the world to the other. As waters give life to the world, so too does Torah give life to the world. As waters are given without cost to the world, so too is Torah given without cost to the world. As waters are given from heaven, so too is Torah given from heaven.... As with water, if one does not know how to swim in it, he will end by drowning, so too with words of Torah. If one does not know how to swim in them and teach them, that person will drown in the end.

(Song of Songs Rabbah 1:2)

Create several of your own personal comparisons of Torah and water, using the model above:

As waters _____, so too is Torah

_____.

As waters _____, so too is Torah

_____.

As waters _____, so too is Torah

_____.

As waters _____, so too is Torah

_____.

As waters _____, so too is Torah

_____.

What did the writers of the Midrash mean when they wrote in Song of Songs Rabbah: "If one does not know how to swim in words of Torah, that person will drown"? Do you agree with this statement?

Text 3: Torah as Fire

It is said that when Jonathan ben Uzziel sat and occupied himself with Torah, every bird that flew over him was instantly incinerated.

(Talmud, Sukkah 28a)

Questions:

How do you explain the statement about ben Uzziel? In what way are words of Torah like fire?

"At God's right hand was a fiery law unto them" (Deuteronomy 33:2). This verse claims that the words of Torah are on fire. As fire was given from heaven, so too were words of Torah given from heaven. Even as fire is life for the world, so words of Torah are life for the world. If one gets close to fire, one can get scorched. If one gets away from the fire, one can get cold. But if one gets near, but not too near, one can enjoy it.

(Sifrei, Deuteronomy, 343)

Questions:

How are words of Torah like fire in this text? How can a person get burned if he or she gets "too close" to Torah? Why would a person get burned by getting too close to Torah?

Fill in these blanks:

As fire _____, so Torah is _____.

As fire _____, so Torah is _____.

As fire _____, so Torah is _____.

As fire _____, so Torah is _____.

As fire _____, so Torah is _____.

Text 4: Study of Torah

Rabbi Eleazar said: "Torah that is studied for its own merits is a Torah of loving-kindness, but Torah that is studied for an ulterior motive is not a Torah of loving-kindness. Some say that Torah that is studied in order to teach is a Torah of loving-kindness, but Torah that is not studied in order to teach is not a Torah of loving-kindness."

(Talmud, Sukkah 49)

Questions:

Can you think of an example of studying Torah for some ulterior motive? Do you agree with the statement that "Torah that is not studied in order to teach is not a Torah of loving-kindness?" What do you think the rabbis meant by this statement?

Rabbi Jonathan said: "If a person persists in the study of Torah while poor, that person will eventually persist in the study of Torah in the midst of wealth. If that person puts aside the study of Torah in the midst of wealth, that person will put aside the study of Torah in poverty."
(Pirke Avot 4:11)

Questions: What do you think is meant by Rabbi Jonathan's statement? How do you think Rabbi Jonathan defines wealth?

Judah ben Tema used to say: "At the age of five, a person is ready for the Bible. At age ten, for the study of Mishnah. At age fifteen, for the study of Talmud."
(Pirke Avot 5:25)

Questions:
What is your opinion of the ages suggested by Judah Ben Tema for Bible and Talmud study? Why do you think it was necessary for him to make this statement in the first place? What ages and kinds of study would you add?

If you want your children to study Torah, study it yourself in their presence. They will follow your example. Otherwise, they will not themselves study Torah, but will simply instruct their children to do so.
(Rabbi Menachem Mendl of Kotzk)

Questions:
What is your opinion of the advice of Menachem Mendl, the Kotzker Rebbe, as he was called? What are some other things that you suggest parents do, so that their children will follow their example? What do your parents offer as examples which you can follow?

How Judaism Differs

The name Torah refers to the first five books of the Hebrew Scriptures, the Jewish Bible. It is also used as a term to include all sacred literature. Christians use the term Old Testament to refer to our Bible, because they have a New Testament which was introduced to fulfill (and supersede) the "old" one. Thus, we should avoid using the term "Old Testament" to describe our Bible. In most Christian editions of the Bible which include the Hebrew Scriptures, the order of the books is a little different.

A Belief System

So what do you conclude about the divine origin of Torah, and its relationship to your life? Some people will argue that if the Torah is not the exact word of God, then why bother with it at all? Can something that is not the exact word of God still reflect the divine? Can it still influence your life?

Godtalk

Torah is more than just a sacred scroll that records the folk history of our people. It is the ongoing dialogue of our people with God. And you are invited, as part of the covenant that was established a long time ago, to join in the dialogue. According to the rabbis of Pirke Avot, the *Shechina* dwells among those who sit and study Torah. It is one of the reasons why *Birkat ha-Mazon* is said at table following meals.

An Exercise

Try using this verse from Psalms as a *kavanna* (a Jewish mantra of sorts), which will prepare you for your day or for those things that you anticipate being difficult: "*B'orekha nereh or*—in Your light do we see light" (Psalm 36:10). Repeat the words over and over again, first aloud and then to yourself, until you have blocked out all other thoughts, until one word flows without interruption into the next. Each time, after you do this, record your thoughts in a journal.

What Can We Believe?

Make a list of those things you believe about the Torah. Use Maimonides' favorite formula to get you started: (Don't worry, to have not so perfect faith is okay too.)

I believe with perfect faith that the Torah_____

_____

I believe with perfect faith that the Torah_____

_____

I believe with perfect faith that the Torah_____

_____

I believe with perfect faith that the Torah_____

_____

I believe with perfect faith that the Torah_____

_____

From Faith to Deeds

Now that we have determined that we believe in the power of Torah as the inspired word of God, how do we translate that into actions? Most people like to point out the Torah's perspective on the things which are listed in the Ten Commandments. These are fairly clear. When the issues are black and white, it is easier to determine their ethical dimensions. However, when things are gray, the ethical ramifications are not so simple.

Take a look at an ethical decision (or unethical decision, as the case may be) which you have made today. It may have been something simple, such as doing your own work for a class or taking credit for something that wasn't quite your own. It may have been about telling a parent part of a story, but leaving out some of the important details necessary to tell the entire story. It may have been about extending yourself to help someone else. What motivated you to make the decision you did? What other choices could you have made? Was it clear, or did you have to think about? Did the position of authorities (like a parent or teacher) have an impact on the decision you made? Were you influenced by peers?

The Spectrum of Jewish Belief: Reform, Conservative, and All the Rest

Reform Judaism teaches that the Torah was divinely inspired and is our most cherished possession as a people. Many Reform Jews believe that God was revealed to the ancient Israelites in the wilderness at a mountain called Sinai. It is for us to ascertain the contents and meaning of the revelation.

While Orthodoxy builds its faith on the absolute belief that God gave every word of the Torah at Mount Sinai, and Reform believes that only the ethical rules were revealed there, Conservative Judaism tries to steer a course between the two. Nearly all Conservative thinkers accept the idea that God revealed the Torah to Israel. But there are some who believe that the revealing of Torah (i.e., revelation) happened only once in history, while others consider revelation to be an ongoing process by which each generation of Jews uncovers more and more of God's word.

Most Conservative thinkers do not believe that God actually spoke each word of the Torah to Moses and Israel. Such thinkers agree with the biblical studies showing that there are different sources in the Bible text, and that Moses could not have been the only writer. So, the majority of Conservative thinkers do not believe that the entire Bible is the word of God. But they do believe that the basic core of Torah, which includes all the important parts, is divine.

Reconstructionism differs greatly from traditional Judaism, because it does not believe that God revealed the Torah to Moses at Sinai. Generally, Reconstructionists accept the thinking of modern biblical scholars, who teach that the Bible is the work of many people in many ages. Mordecai Kaplan, founder of the Reconstructionist movement, wrote that the Torah is not the record of God's word to people. Rather it is the result of people's search for God. Whenever a person discovers a religious truth or great moral idea, it is a revelation of God's will.

What do you think happened on Mount Sinai?

PRINCIPLE NINE

The Dialogue of Torah Across the Generations

I believe with perfect faith that this Torah will not be changed, and that there will never be any other law from the Creator, blessed be Your name.

Getting Started: Some Background

According to Jewish tradition, the Torah was revealed at Mount Sinai. While many people think that this revelation took place just before the Israelites entered the land of Canaan, the experience at Sinai took place early in their journey from Egypt to the Promised Land. Some scholars believe that Torah was progressively revealed to the Jewish people during their forty years of travel in the desert, and was not given at a specific place and time. Whatever the case, according to Maimonides—who is reflecting traditional Jewish thought—that revelation, the Torah as we know it, will last us through to eternity. We like to argue that revelation began at Sinai and continues until now. The only reason that we do not always realize that revelation is still taking place, that God continues to speak to us, is that there is too much noise in the world for us to hear God's voice. If this is the case, then the Torah has to be able to provide insight into questions that it never anticipated. What can we do to limit the noise, the interference, so that we can hear God's voice more clearly?

A Ready Reference

As far as the rabbis are concerned, two Torahs were given at Mount Sinai. The first one was written down. It is called the *Torah she-bikh-tav*. The second one was not written down. Instead, it was given in oral form, and passed down through the generations until it was finally written down in the form of the Talmud. It is called *Torah she-be-al peh*. Thus, it is Torah in this inclusive sense that Maimonides believes will not be changed or added to.

The term Torah is also used to refer to general Jewish knowledge, the wide array of sacred literature that extends beyond the written and oral law. We even go as far as to say that what one has to teach in a Jewish context may be called Torah, so that we may say, "This is the Torah I would like to teach you." Construct a similar sentence in which you might use the word Torah without referring to the written or oral law.

_____

_____

_____

What We Believe

The Torah is more than just the primary sacred text of the Jewish people. In it is contained the essential values of Judaism as understood by the rabbis. Thus, every aspect of it is important. Scholars study it so that they may uncover new layers of meaning each time they enter its pages. There are those who say that music is made from the spaces between the notes. Likewise, even the spaces between the letters have something to teach us.

We like to say that Torah does not really exist until we enter into dialogue with it. What does this phrase mean?

_____

_____

If this is the case, then how do you enter into a dialogue with the text? We enter the text by becoming one with the characters and events that are described in the Torah as the story of the Jewish people unfolds. In other words, we become the Torah. Take Abraham or Sarah for example. Make their struggle your struggle. Live with them for a period of time. Imagine yourselves as them (since a part of them lives within your soul—and maybe even your gene pool).

Many of us do not believe that the Torah was given as we know it at Mount Sinai. Instead, we recognize the presence of human hands in the telling and editing of the stories in the text. But this does not change its transformative power for our lives.

The Torah is also called a blueprint for the world. In other words, God consulted the Torah when creating this world. The early rabbis debated this idea among themselves. Some said that the Torah was one of the six or seven things created just prior to the creation of the world. Others suggested that God took council with the Torah before creating the world. How do you think that worked if the Torah was not given to the Israelites until Sinai? Let's take a look at what some of the great Jewish philosophers believed about the preexistence of the Torah.

Saadia Gaon rejected the idea of a preexistent Torah because it contradicted the notion of *creatio ex nihilo* (creation out of nothing). He takes Proverbs 8:22 ("God created me at the beginning of the course, as the first of God's work of old.") quite literally, arguing that it simply means that God created the world wisely.

Judah ben Barzaillai of Barcelona asked a very basic question of this theory. If the Torah existed before the creation of the world, then where did God keep the Torah? He suggested that perhaps the Torah only existed as an idea in the divine mind. In the end, he argued that the notion of a preexistent Torah emerged out of great love for the Torah, but was not based in any reality. Like so many other rabbinic ideas, it is only a metaphor.

Abraham ibn Ezra argued against the idea from the perspective of time. Since time is an accident of motion, and there was no motion prior to creation, then the Torah could not have existed prior to the creation of the world. He called the theory a metaphoric riddle.

Judah Halevi took a different position. He suggested that the Torah's existence prior to the creation of the world must be seen through the lens of philosophic teleology (a fancy term meaning that the end or goal is the important focus). God created the world in order to reveal the Torah. If this is the purpose of creation, then the Torah, in that sense, preceded the creation of the world.

Moses Maimonides did not discuss this idea at all in his great work, the *Moreh Nevukhim* (*Guide for the Perplexed*). However, he did discuss the origin of the Torah from the perspective of the unique prophecy of Moses. Since the discussion of a throne of glory (which was discussed in the *Guide*) and the idea that the Torah existed prior to the world are both esoteric and rather controversial, they should be left to the individual to interpret. Even in this principle (no. 9), Maimonides does not discuss the origin of the Torah or its preexistence.

Isaac ibn Latif maintained that the Torah precedes the world in rank rather than in time. He bases his argument on the aggadic statements about the preexistence of the throne of glory and the Torah's preexistence to the throne of glory. The Torah exists in the upper world of the wisdom, or intellect, but the throne of glory exists in the middle world (with the celestial spheres). Both stand above our lower world which includes changing elements.

For the kabbalists, the preexistence of the world became an important principle. Some argued that the Torah was God's wisdom, which stood as the second of the ten *sefirot* of emanation (a complicated, theoretical, mystical construction of God's presence is manifest in the world). Others identified the Torah with the sixth *sefirah* (*Tiferet*, or beauty), and still others called it *Malkhut* (sovereignty), the tenth *sefirah*. Following is a schematic of the *sefirot*.

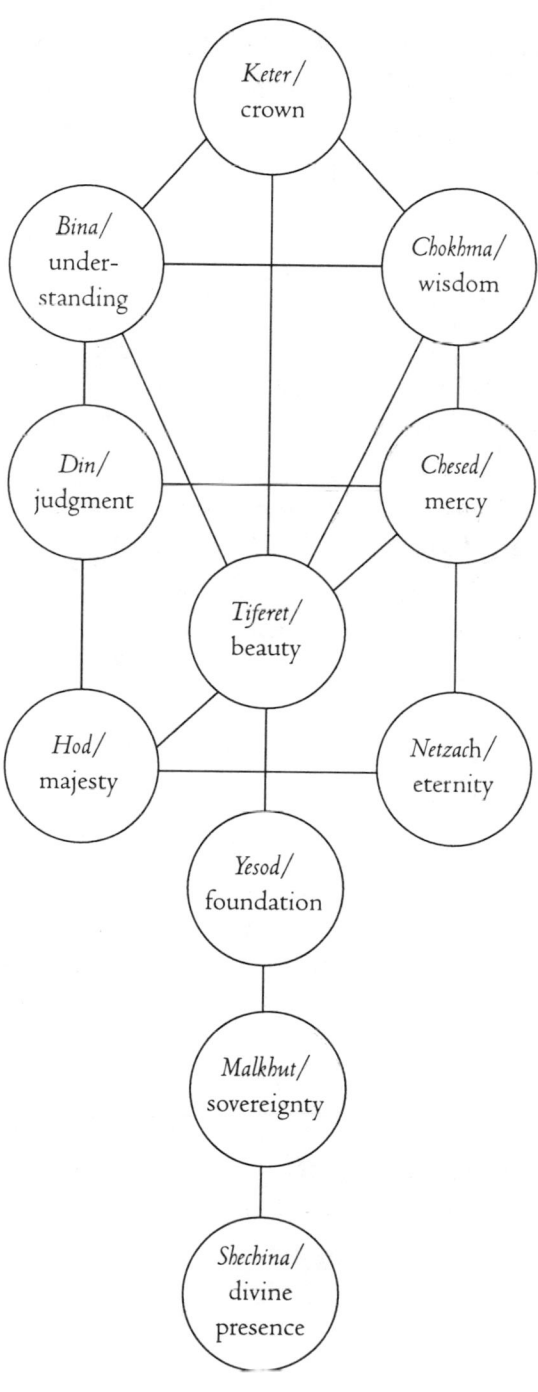

Hasdai Crescas took the preexistence of the Torah literally, as chronology. By way of a rather complicated philosophical argument (using what is called a metonymy), Crescas suggests that the purpose of the Torah is love. Since the final cause of an object chronologically precedes it, the purpose of the Torah chronologically preceded the world. He uses a statement from the Talmud to support his claim: "Were it not for the Torah (given out of love), the world would not have come into existence" (Talmud, Pesachim 68b).

Joseph Albo studied with Crescas, but his position on the preexistence of the Torah is based on the works of Judah Halevi. Albo believed that humanity exists for the sake of Torah. And everything in the world exists for the sake of humanity. So he reasoned that Torah preceded the world because the final cause has to precede other causes.

Franz Rosenzweig in his *Star of Redemption* reacted to the intellectualist interpretation of the Torah by the German rabbis. He considered it absurd to try to justify the preexistence of the Torah in historical terms. As an existentialist, he looked for his own proof in the Aggadah. He wrote simply, "No doubt the Torah, both written and oral, was given to Moses on Sinai, but was it not created before the creation of the world? Written against a background of shining fire in letters of somber flame? And was not the world created for its sake?"

Now that you have read what some of the great Jewish philosophers have said, what do you think?

An Exercise

Do you ever get a funny feeling when you meet someone for the first time? As if you had met that person before. Some people like to say, "I remember you from Sinai." Are they serious or are they making a joke? As a metaphysical principle, according to Jewish tradition, we were all there at the giving of Torah. We believe it. This is part of what is called the historical memory of the Jewish people. We have lived through all of Jewish history with our ancestors. But the present challenge is to reach back into our memories in order to recall the event of *matan Torah* (the giving of Torah). Close your eyes. Think back to your earliest memory as a child. Focus on it. Try to bring it back to life. Now, reach back beyond it. Consider the events that may have brought your family to this country, to the community in which you live. Now, travel back through the events in Jewish history that are most familiar to you. They are all buried in the back of your mind (just like many of the answers to that math test that you just can't remember). Keep going back as far as you can until you reach the Sinai desert. Don't try to remember the entire episode. Instead, focus on one item. It may be as simple as how the sand felt beneath your feet or the heat of the midday desert sun. After you do this exercise numerous times, you will begin to be able to put together the various parts of this memory and reconstruct your memory of the Sinai experience in its entirety.

Extending the Principle of Faith

Even among those who argue that the Torah was not divinely revealed and that it includes the work of human hands, they still look for its guidance with regard to questions that were not and could not have been considered in the year 1250 B.C.E. or even later, during the rabbinic period, when the Talmud was completed (in the fifth century C.E.). During the medieval period, scholars prepared law codes which attempted to organize the many laws of the Talmud so that they could be used to answer pressing questions of the day. Maimonides prepared the most comprehensive law code called the *Mishneh Torah*. Later, Joseph Caro developed the *Shulchan Arukh*, which is still used by observant Jews today. However, it became clear that more needed to be done. People began to ask questions of rabbis. Often, these questions were posed by communal rabbis to scholars who lived in other communities. Their written responses evolved into a literature of questions and answers called *responsa*. Regardless of the religious movement, the process continues today. The Conservative Movement is guided by the Law Committee of the Rabbinical Assembly, and the Reform Movement is guided by the Committee on Responsa of the Central Conference of American Rabbis. It might be said that the process is more important today as the world becomes more and more complicated. Orthodox Jews generally look to individual rabbinic authorities for legal decisions.

Here are excerpts from one of the most recent responsa of the (Conservative) Rabbinical Assembly's Law Committee. It is in answer to the question: Is tattooing one's body permitted? Does it preclude taking part in synagogue rituals, or from being buried in a Jewish cemetery?

Answer: The prohibition of tattooing is found in the Torah: You shall not make gashes in your flesh for the dead, or incise any marks on yourselves: I am God. [Leviticus 19:28] It is the second part of this verse from which we derive the general prohibition against tattooing. From the outset, there is disagreement about what precisely makes tattooing a prohibited act. The *Mishnah* states that it is the lasting and permanent nature of tattooing which makes it a culpable act:

If a man wrote on his skin pricked-in writing ... he is not culpable unless he writes it and pricks it in with ink or eye-paint or anything that leaves a lasting mark. [Mishneh Makkot 3:6]

But Rabbi Simeon ben Judah disagrees, and says that it is the inclusion of God's name which makes it a culpable act:

Rabbi Simeon ben Judah says, in the name of Rabbi Simeon: He is not culpable unless he writes there the name [of a god], for it is written, "Or incise any marks on yourselves, I am God." [Mishneh Makkot 3:6]

The *Gemara* goes on to debate whether it is the inclusion of God's name or a pagan deity that makes it a culpable act.

Maimonides clearly sees the origin of this prohibition in an act of idolatry. He includes it in his section concerning idolatry and then explicitly states: "This was a custom among the pagans who marked themselves for idolatry..." [*Mishneh Torah*, Laws of Idolatry]

Regardless of the exact limits of this prohibition, over time the rabbis clearly extended the prohibition to include all tattooing.

In our day, the prohibition against all forms of tattooing regardless of their intent, should be maintained. In addition to the fact that Judaism has a long history of distaste for tattoos, tattooing becomes even more distasteful in a contemporary secular society that is constantly challenging the Jewish concept that we are created *b'tzelem Elohim* (in God's image), and that our bodies are to be viewed as a precious gift on loan from God, to be entrusted into our care, and not our personal property to do with as we choose. Voluntary tattooing, even if not done for idolatrous purposes, expresses a negation of this fundamental Jewish perspective.

As tattoos become more popular in contemporary society, there is a need to reinforce the prohibition against tattooing in our communities, and to counterbalance it with education regarding the traditional concept that we are created in God's image. But, however distasteful we may find the practice, there is no basis for restricting burial from Jews who violate this prohibition or even limiting their participation in synagogue ritual....

New laser technology has raised the possibility of removing what was once irremovable. To date, this procedure is painful, long, and very expensive. However, it will probably not be long before the process is refined to the point where it will not be painful, overly involved, or very expensive. At such a time, it might be appropriate for the law committee to consider whether removal of tattoos should become a requirement of *teshuvah*, conversion, or burial.

The prohibition of tattooing throughout the halakhic literature deals only with personal, voluntary tattooing. With respect to the reprehensible practice of the Nazis, who marked the arms of Jews with tattooed numbers and letters during the Shoah, the *Shulkhan Arukh* (Code of Jewish Law) makes it clear that those who bear these tattoos are blameless: If it [the tattoo] was done in the flesh of another, the one to whom it was done is blameless. [*Shulkhan Arukh*, Yoreh De'ah 180:2]

Tattoos which are used in cancer treatment or any similar medical procedure to permanently mark the body for necessary life-saving treatment are also not included in the prohibition against tattooing.[*Shulchan Arukh*, Yoreh De'ah 180:3]

The prohibition against tattoos applies only to permanent marks to the skin. Therefore, hand stamps or other popular children's decorations which mimic tattoos and paint the skin in a nonpermanent manner cannot be included under the prohibition of tattooing.

Because the Torah is so central to Judaism, it is handled in a special way. For example, whenever the Torah is taken from the ark or raised up, the entire community stands. This follows the logic that since individuals are required to stand in the presence of those learned in Torah (as Leviticus 19:32 is understood), then how much more should individuals stand before the Torah itself (Talmud, Kiddushin 33b). As with many rituals there is usually a practical logic, as well as a spiritual logic, explaining why the Torah is handled in the way that it is when we read from it publicly (and simulate the revelation of Torah at Sinai). (For example, for *hakafot*, or Torah processional, rather simply.) When the Torah was taken from the ark, people wanted to express their love of the sacred text by handling it and kissing it. As congregations grew in size, this was no longer so simple as a formal circuit evolved.

Let's make a list of some of the principles of handling the Torah which reflect both the practical logic and spiritual logic. We'll get you started.

1. Never turn your back on the Torah. Follow it with your eyes, and by turning your body towards it as it makes its way around the sanctuary. (This is another reason why people often descend the *bima* backwards.)

2. You are permitted to talk during most of the service (unless you get yelled at by the rabbi, your teacher, or an usher), but it is considered inappropriate to talk while the Torah is being read (since it is God who is speaking, and you would be "dissing" God).

3. During the processional, carry the Torah in your right arm. Others in the processional should follow the one holding the Torah.

4. As the Torah passes, always take a step towards it. (Some congregations form two rows around the periphery of the sanctuary so that the Torah may pass between them.) Don't wait for the Torah to come to you. And if you can't reach the Torah because there are too many people impeding your progress, simply bow slightly as it passes.

5._____

6._____

7._____

8._____

9._____

10._____

Personalizing the Principle of Faith

If God is not planning on providing us with any additional Torah—so Maimonides declares—then how do we go about using the Torah we have to inform our lives? How can the Torah provide us with insight and direction when we have to make difficult decisions? Have you ever turned to the Torah for help when you were faced with a difficult problem? Describe how you used the Torah below.

_____

_____

_____

_____

_____

What were the circumstances which motivated you to turn to the Torah for guidance?

Now comes the hard question which people are unwilling to ask. It is too easy to reply with some sarcastic answer. So try to avoid the temptation. It is what we call the question before the question: Why turn to the Torah, at all, for guidance? To answer the question honestly, you have to reach deep inside yourself, and probe your Jewish soul and self.

Textual Encounters

Here are some texts that relate to Torah and Torah study. After reading each try to answer the question(s) that follow:

Text I:

Rabbi Menachem Mendl of Kotzk taught: If you want your children to study Torah, study it yourself in their presence. They will surely follow your example.

Question:

Do you believe that adults are role models for children. In what way are your parents role models for you?

Text 2:

If you review your Torah study while strolling and carelessly interrupt your studies to remark, "what a beautiful tree," or "what a lovely field," you are considered as having committed a capital offense. (Pirke Avot 3:9)

Question:

What do you think the rabbis meant when they made this statement? Were they exaggerating, or is one to understand this statement literally?

Text 3:

Torah is acquired through forty-eight virtues: by study, attentiveness, orderly speech, by an understanding heart, by a perceptive heart, by awe, fear, humility, joy, by ministering to the sages, by cleaving to colleagues, by acute discussion with students, by calmness in study, by study of Bible and Mishnah, by a minimum of business, by a minimum of sleep, by a minimum of small talk, by a minimum of worldly pursuits, by patience, by a generous heart, by trust in the sages, by acceptance of suffering, by knowing one's place, by contentment with one's lot, by guarding one's speech, by taking no personal credit, by being beloved, by loving God, by loving all creatures, by loving charitable deeds, by loving rectitude, by loving reproof, by shunning honor, by not boasting of one's learning, by not delighting in rendering decisions, by sharing the burden with one's fellow, by influencing your fellow to virtue, by setting your fellow on the path of truth, by setting your fellow on the path of peace, by concentrating on one's studies, by asking and answering questions, by absorbing knowledge and contributing to it, by studying in order to teach and perform mitzvot, by sharpening the wisdom of one's teacher, by being precise in transmitting what one has learned, by quoting the source. (Pirke Avot 6:6)

Questions:

Of the virtues listed in this list of forty-eight, what would be your choice for the five most important virtues? What virtues would you add to this list? What virtues do you think teachers admire in their students?

How Judaism Differs

While Christianity accepts the Hebrew Bible (even though it calls it the Old Testament, which is superseded by the New Testament or New

Covenant), the notion of the Torah which animates Judaism does not exist. Even the way in which the story of creation (in Genesis) is often translated by Christians makes the idea of Torah, as Torah, irrelevant.

From Faith to Deeds

If the Torah is primarily the way we understand God's communication with the Jewish people, then the performance of *mitzvot* is the primary way by which we can respond to that communication. However, each movement understands *mitzvot* a little differently. But all of the movements suggest that we have to start somewhere, one *mitzvah* at a time. For you, which *mitzvah* speaks as a response to Maimonides' ninth principle? And how are you going to go about making it part of your religious life, as part of your commitment to Confirmation? (For a list of all 613 commandments which Maimonides assembled, take a look at our *"How To" Handbook for Jewish Living.*)

Godtalk

The Torah is the centralized form of God's public communication with us. But God also speaks to us in private. (Sometimes that is recorded in the Torah also.) What do you think is the relationship between God's public communication through the Torah and God's private communication with us?

What Can We Believe?

Okay, here is the big question: Can we believe that the Torah existed prior to the creation of the world, and that it is the channel through which God communicates with the world? If you do believe this, as did Moses Maimonides, then how would you construct a philosophical argument so that you might explain the principle to others? And once you decide, how does your decision affect your Jewish practice?

The Spectrum of Jewish Belief: Reform, Conservative, and All the Rest

For Reform Jews, Torah represents the wide body of Jewish knowledge. And revelation itself is ongoing. It is not finite, and includes the far reaches of human discovery. Thus, Maimonides' position cannot be challenged. Orthodox Judaism accepts the Torah as God-given. And God is omniscient. Thus, if it does not provide us with guidance for a contemporary issue, then this reflects our shortcoming, rather than an expression of the limitation of the Torah itself. A simpler way of putting it is, that Orthodoxy tries to make the world fit Torah, but Progressive Judaism strives to make Torah fit the world.

While Orthodox Judaism builds its faith on the absolute belief that God gave every word of the Torah at Mount Sinai, and Reform Judaism believes that, for the most part, the ethical rules were revealed therein, Conservative Judaism tries to steer a course between the two. Nearly all Conservative thinkers accept the idea that God revealed the Torah to Israel. But there are some who believe that the revealing of the Torah, or revelation, happened only once in history, while others consider revelation to be an ongoing process by which each generation of Jews uncovers more and more of God's word.

Most Conservative thinkers do not believe that God actually spoke each word of Torah to Moses and Israel. In fact, biblical studies have shown that there are different sources in the Bible text, and that Moses could not have been the only writer. So the majority of Conservative thinkers do not believe that the entire Bible is the word of God. But they do believe that the basic core of Torah, that is, the important parts, may be said to be divine.

Reconstructionism differs greatly from traditional Judaism, because it does not believe that God revealed the Torah to Moses at Sinai. The Reconstructionists generally accept the thinking of modern biblical scholars, who teach that the Bible is the work of many people in many ages. Rabbi Mordecai Kaplan, the founder of the Reconstructionist movement, wrote that the Bible is not the record of God's word to people, but of humanity's search for God. Whenever we discover a religious truth or great moral idea, it is, for Reconstructionists, a revelation of God's will.

PRINCIPLE TEN

Divine Vision

I believe with perfect faith that the Creator, praised be Your name, knows every deed of the human race and all of their thoughts, as it is said, "It is You who fashions all of their hearts, who pays attention to all their deeds."

Getting Started: Some Background

Why should God bother to pay attention to everything we do? As with a parent (remember principle no. 1: God is the Creator of all of humanity), God takes an interest in everything we do. Unlike our parents, however, who try to influence us even when they are not with us, God is constantly with us. Rabbi Olitzky once had a teacher who made him feel like he was his only student. The remarkable thing was that others felt the same way about this teacher. *L'havdil* (that's a Hebrew expression that separates the context of our thoughts from one another), we feel like our relationship with God is unique (and it is), yet we know that God has a special relationship with millions of other people at the same time.

Do you have a teacher who makes you feel that way?

Have you ever been in the audience of a speaker, or in the classroom of a teacher, or in the congregation with a rabbi, where you felt that the speaker/teacher/rabbi was speaking directly to you—and nearly everyone else was oblivious to your dialogue?

Do you ever feel that way about God?

Do you remember Johnny Carson's "Great Carnac" routine on the

Tonight Show—before Jay Leno? It was a simple gag. Someone would prepare a set of statements (answers to questions), and place them individually in sealed envelopes. Carson, as Carnac, would hold the envelopes one
at a time to his head, then ask the question that the sealed statement was
supposed to answer. Afterwards, he would read the answer, which usually
drew much hilarity. Try it for yourself. It ain't easy—even as a comic routine. Maimonides argues in principle no. 10 that God knows the questions
and the answers.

There are also those who feel that they know what others are thinking,
who can sense events that are happening, even at a distance. While we cannot always explain this phenomenon, we believe it. Following Rabbi Shira
Millgrom, a spiritual leader of Congregation Kol Ami in White Plains,
New York, we like to call these windows, because they open us up to the
unknown, to the world beyond the rational (what is often referred to as
the metarational). These windows allow us a glimpse into a world beyond
the edges of everyday thinking.

Have you or anyone you know ever had such an experience? Describe
it below.

_____

_____

_____

_____

_____

Perhaps this possibility is a result of the divine spark which rests inside
each and every one of us. Maybe it is something that can be nurtured, if
we are willing to pay attention to this voice inside our soul which wants to
be heard.

A Ready Reference

There are many attributes that are traditionally assigned to God. Among them is the ability to be all-knowing, what is called omniscience. It is like having a divine video camera with a microphone focused on you all the time, wherever you go. Some consider this claim impossible. Others find comfort in it. Still others use it as a measuring stick for moral judgment. In other words, you may think that nobody but you knows what you do or what you think, but God sees it all. The challenge remains: If God sees all that you do, does God also influence what you say or do?

What We Believe

Unlike with so many other principles, there is a not really a continuum of belief with regard to God's omniscience. For some people, the existence of a multiplicity of opinions about particular principles is discomforting. For others, it is encouraging, because it embraces the views of more people, making them feel comfortable as Jews. While there may be some difference of opinion concerning this principle, the real difference of opinion enters the conversation when theologians begin to draw conclusions from God's ability to know and see all. What conclusions are you prepared to consider? We have listed some of them which represent the wide spectrum of Jewish thought.

1. Because God is all-seeing, God can anticipate events before they occur.

2. Because God is all-seeing, God can anticipate events before they occur. However, individuals have free will.

3. Because God is all-seeing, God can intervene in events before they occur.

4. God's omniscience is a metaphor of sorts. God knows all that is possible to know, because God is the creator of all (see principle no. 1).

But God is unable (or perhaps not interested) in keeping tabs on each and every individual at all times.

5. Just because God can see all that goes on in the world does not mean that God can do anything about it. God created the world, set it in motion, and now has to live with the consequences of human deeds and misdeeds.

6.

7.

8.

9.

10.

An Exercise

Think back to a decision which you may have made within the last month. Not a simple decision such as "What movie should I go to?" or "Which pair of jeans should I wear?" Rather, consider a decision that required some moral judgment. Did you have to think about whether it was an appropriate action or not? (Often when you really have to think through whether the action is moral or not, it is probably because it is not the right thing to do, and you are better off not doing it!) What role did "nobody knows what I am doing" play in your decision? Did you even consider that God may indeed be fully aware of what you decided to do? Did that consideration have an impact on your decision?

According to moral development theorists (those who plot out the ability to make moral decisions over the lifespan of the individual according to one's age and development), our early moral decisions are guided by people who influence our lives as figures of authority. So, our parents provide us with initial guidance. In other words, as children, we look to parents and other people in authority to help us make our moral decisions. That's why such role modeling is so important for younger children. As we grow older—into adolescence—we begin to reject such authority, and look to the acceptance of our peers as a way of measuring moral decisions. As a result, the makeup of a peer group is very important to rebellious teenagers (who are probably all of you who are reading this book, preparing for Confirmation). As we get older—into college-age years and beyond, or, some say, not until the late twenties or early thirties—we begin to morally reason on an abstract basis, and have the ability to make these decisions on our own. (The truth is that whether we have the ability or not, we still must make these decisions.) Some people, argue these theorists, never reach the stage where they can come to a moral decision on their own. So what do you think? How do you go about making decisions? Here is one for you:

It's a party. You are invited, and attend, not knowing what to expect. There are lots of people there, some you know, some you don't know. But you hang with your own group. There are no parents at home. Someone decides to raid the liquor cabinet, and invites you to join in. How do you respond? More importantly, how do go about making your decision? And does God see the whole thing, and guide you into making the right decision?

Let's try another one. It's your first date with the girl/boy of your dreams. She/he wants to have sex. You're not ready, not even sure it's right. How do you respond? More important, how do go about making your decision? And does God see the whole thing, and guide you into making the right decision?

Extending the Principle of Faith

If God knows and sees all, then we have an obligation to try to figure out "what God wants me to do?" This is a question that reflects individual moral decisions. But it is also a general question. Consider the way the prophet Micah asked the question. He thought that the answer would offer guidance to individuals. Micah said, "What does God require of me? Only to do justly, to love mercy, and to walk humbly with God" (6:8).

Rabbi Rami Shapiro extended Micah's question. Rabbi Shapiro contends that these three rubrics can be divided into three categories of practice. The first section is *asot mishpat*—do justly. This obligates us to these mitzvot.

Eco-*kashrut* (ethical consumption): Our diet has to be tied to the highest ethical and environmental standards.

Tzedaka (just use of finances): What we do with our money, as well as how we earn it, has an impact on self and society.

Tikkun olam (perfecting the world): As a partner of God, we have a responsibility to support organizations which will make the world more just and holy.

Micah's second category is *ahavat chesed*—loving-kindness. According to Rabbi Shapiro, these four mitzvot provide us with the path to respond to Micah's second obligation.

Gemilut chasadim (acts of kindness): Seek out opportunities to do kindness everyday.

Lashon hara (avoiding hateful speech): Use words to heal rather than hurt.

Hachnasat orchim (embracing the stranger): Cultivate openness and friendship.

Shalom bayit (peaceful household): Celebrate family and all it represents.

In response to Micah's third category, *hatznaya lechet*—walking humbly with God, Rabbi Shapiro suggests five spiritual practices:

Shabbat (a day of mindfulness): Find in Shabbat a refuge and a delight.

Limud Torah (Learning Torah): Reclaim the deep insights of timeless tales and eternal virtues through the study of sacred text.

Hitbodedut (God encounter): Spiritual practice is all about opening up to God through daily prayer and meditation.

Teshuva (perfecting oneself): Constantly measure your actions, and seek to improve them.

Berakhot (the way of wonder): Cultivate gratitude, grace, and awe by honoring the "ordinary" miracles of everyday life.

Personalizing the Principle of Faith

As we read the Torah, we see that there are specific words that are used to announce important things which follow. When we encounter them, we pay special attention to what follows. For example, in the early chapters of Genesis, we find Adam and Eve in the Garden. Once they have eaten from the tree of knowledge of good and evil, God calls out to Adam, "*Ayeka?*" (i.e., "Where are you?"). God knew where Adam was. God was really asking something more significant. It was as if God said to Adam, "Do you know where you are?" Then, Adam responds "Hineni" (i.e., "I am here.") And you know something significant is about to happen. This Hineni is the same phrase that is used when Isaac calls out to his father, Abraham, as they together make their way toward Moriah. Abraham responds to Isaac "Hineni," or "I am here."

This phrase has become somewhat of a moral imperative. In a rather poignant contemporary Jewish folk song, singer/songwriter Doug Cotler asks whether we will have the moral courage to say *Hineni* when God calls us to action.

Textual Encounters

The rabbis wrote in Pirke Avot: "All is foreseen, but freedom of choice is given" (3:19). This seems like an oxymoron, that is, a seemingly self-contradictory phrase. How can both be possible? Unpack the text, and see how you can affirm the text. Try explaining it on your own. Rabbi Akiva used this verse to substantiate the statement: "I call heaven and earth to witness against you this day, that I have set before you life and death, blessing and curse. Therefore, choose life" (Deuteronomy 30:19). Why would Rabbi Akiva use this verse? What verse would you select?

Above the ark in many synagogues is the phrase (usually in Hebrew): "Know before Whom you stand." Obviously, the verse refers to God. It reminds us that, whatever we do, wherever we go, God is there watching. Why would this text be chosen for the ark?

Choose a different one or write your own, below.

_____

_____

_____

How Judaism Differs

The diversity that marks various segments of the Jewish community with regard to this principle is represented equally in the non-Jewish community. Interview five members of the community, each representing the various movements, including your own. Remember to include someone who is not affiliated with any religious movement in the community. Ask them for their opinion. Do they agree with this principle? Do they think that the movement with which they affiliate affirms the principle?

From Faith to Deeds

If God knows all that we think and do, then our actions should reflect that kind of awareness. How would your behavior change if you were to ask yourself prior to each action, "Would God be pleased with me were I to do this?" Rabbi Laura Geller encourages us to ask a different question, particularly as we face moral questions with regard to sexuality. She says that we should ask whether what we are about to do may be considered holy? If we are not able to classify the act as holy, then we should not engage in it. Spend this week trying this practice as a regular part of your daily routine.

At the end of the week, refine the question, and practice so that you can carry the practice forward.

Godtalk

Since God knows what we are doing, this knowledge provides us with the opportunity to enter into dialogue with God about what it is we are doing. What can you do to make God a partner in your actions—and your reflections on those actions?

What Can We Believe?

We can believe whatever we choose to believe about God's omniscience. But what we believe has an impact on what we do. This belief helps to nurture our relationship with the divine. How does your affirmation or rejection of this principle make an impact on your relationship with God?

The Spectrum of Jewish Belief: Reform, Conservative, and All the Rest

Regarding the principle of divine omniscience, there is probably little division among the various Jewish religious movements. Yet, within each of these movements there may be disagreement. Some may argue that God knows what we do, but that God can do nothing about it. Others will suggest that because God knows all that we do, there is room for divine intervention. Such is the case with Orthodox Judaism.

PRINCIPLE ELEVEN

The System of Reward and Punishment

I believe with perfect faith that the Creator, praised be Your name, rewards those that keep Your mitzvot, and punishes those who transgress them.

Getting Started: Some Background

Principle no. 11 is crucial to an understanding of the Jewish religious psyche, but it is extremely controversial. As a result, people prefer to avoid it when discussing the basic principles of Judaism. Maybe this is one of the reasons why Maimonides placed it toward the end of his set of thirteen basic principles. Perhaps he felt that if the first ten principles helped provide a foundation for this eleventh principle, it would be better accepted. He may even have believed that it was a natural outgrowth of what preceded. As students for Confirmation, it is important to explore such controversial principles so that you can determine for yourself whether, or to what extent, you are prepared to *confirm* them. This principle presents a slight spin on one of the ideas which the rabbis introduced into the Jewish community as a part of a set of ideas that challenged the authority of the priests and the preeminence of the written law. They argued that the oral law was given on Sinai alongside the written law. Both are considered Torah. The rabbis also felt that there were some specific principles that were not self-evident in the written law, but were made explicit in the oral law. In the case of this principle, Maimonides has rewritten the concept slightly, but the basic idea remains the same: God rewards those who do good (reworked by Maimonides as "those that keep Your *mitzvot*"), and punishes those who do evil (restated by Maimonides as "those who transgress them"). In order to counter those who may suggest that our experience does not bear out this statement, the rabbis suggest that our perspective of the system of reward and punishment should not be restricted to this world. Instead, one has to consider this world *and* the next world as part of one complete unit. Thus, people are either rewarded or punished in this world and, more often, the next world. (More on the afterlife and the world beyond in principles 12 and 13.)

Some scholars argue that the rabbis championed this idea as part of an innovative plan to wrestle communal authority away from the priests. Following the destruction of the Temple, this became a moot point. The priests no longer had a precinct within which to work and act as an authority base. But the question continues to hound us: Why do we see good people suffer and evil ones prosper if what Maimonides claims holds true? And what can we do about it, if anything?

A Ready Reference

What are *mitzvot*? According to traditional Judaism, *mitzvot* are those behaviors that God commanded us to do or prohibited us from doing. Simply put, what makes them commandments (and therefore incumbent upon us to do them) is that they are dictated by the Commander, namely God. According to tradition, there are 613 *mitzvot*. (For a complete listing, see our *"How To" Handbook for Jewish Living*.) These were culled from the Torah, and explicated in the Talmud. If you were to read the entire Torah, *parasha* by *parasha*, you would be able to discover all of them. Some are clearly indicated. Others are not so self-evident. Beginning in the medieval period, scholars prepared volumes dedicated to the task of detailing each *mitzvah* as it appeared in the Torah. For an excellent example of this literature, take a look at *Sefer ha-Chinukh* (literally, Book of Education), which is now available in English translation.

How would you define *mitzvah*?

What is the relationship that *mitzvot* have to your life?

What We Believe

Some scholars argue that this principle was laid out for primitive people who needed to have mapped for them the exact consequences of good and evil behavior. Others simply understand the text to mean that every person's action in life will result in a consequence, and that one should therefore be careful about what one is about to do before doing it. It is the Jewish approach to what modern theorists call moral development. Rabbi Olitzky likes to say to people, particularly to his own sons, when they are complaining about someone else's behavior, "He (or she) has to live with himself (or herself). That's punishment enough. Just be glad that you don't have to."

Both of us want to believe that Maimonides is correct about this closed system of reward and punishment, but it would force us to make a matter of faith something that seems to stand in opposition to what we regularly experience. Some say that the reward of doing a *mitzvah* is the *mitzvah* itself. Perhaps because the *mitzvah* has the potential of bringing us closer to God. And this is the way we deal with it. We accept Maimonides' principle, although we do not fully understand how it plays out in this world *or* the next. Therefore, we are willing to continue our unrelenting search. Moreover, we are committed to it. We are willing to continue to look for justice, that is, those specific times when goodness is rewarded and evil is punished. Because of our faith in God, we can live with this uncertainty. Can you?

An Exercise

Take a look at this week's Torah portion. Read it through in its entirety, one verse at a time. As you read each verse, make a list of those *mitzvot* that you think are outlined in the portion. Cross out any *mitzvot* that you are unable to fulfill (generally because they are restricted to the archaic sacrificial cult, or limited to the land of Israel). Put two lines through those that your religious movement has rejected as a matter of principle. (This is particularly important for Reform Jews.) Then, put a checkmark next to those that you follow.

Now comes the hard part. Of those *mitzvot* which you do follow, how are you rewarded for following them? How do you think that you will be rewarded for following them? And of those which you don't follow, how will you be punished for not following them?

Extending the Principle of Faith

Most *mitzvot* have a specific measure. As a matter of fact, the rabbis tell us that we are not permitted to increase (so that we should not presume ourselves to become overly pious) or decrease (so that we should not be considered superficial) this measurement. However, there are a set of *mitzvot* that may be done without regard to specific measure. (They are included among the study materials in the weekday morning worship service.) We can just keep doing them. They include study and honoring parents, among others. There is one among the list which literally reads, "accompanying the dead." We have to provide a proper burial for those who die. This *mitzvah* is considered a *mitzvah shel chesed v'emet*, or a really honest *mitzvah*. Why? Because there is no possibility that you are doing this *mitzvah* in anticipation of reaping a benefit from the one for whom the *mitzvah* is performed. The *mitzvot* mentioned in Peah 1:1 include: the corner of the field, the first-fruits, the pilgrimage offerings, the practice of kindness, and the study of Torah. The other *mitzvot* cited are from the Talmud, Shabbat 127a, and they are the things "of which a man enjoys the fruits in this world, while the principal remains for the individual in the hereafter." They include: honoring father and mother, the practice of kindness, early, morning and evening *beit midrash* attendance, kindness to strangers, visiting the ill, dowering the bride, attending the dead to the grave, *kavanna*, peacemaking and preeminently, study of the Torah.

Within a system of reward and punishment, our motivations must be considered. Why indeed do a particular *mitzvah*? Name one *mitzvah* that you regularly do. Why do you do it?

Extend Deuteronomy 11:13–21 (the second paragraph of the *Shema*) to caring for the earth and the environment. If the earth is cared for, then it will yield its fruits. If it is abused, then its produce will not be favorable.

This text from the Torah is contained in our worship service, twice daily. It clearly spells out a specific set of rewards and punishments with regard to the care of the earth. But it is not restricted to individuals. Instead, it is really a directive from God to all of us. If we care for the earth and the environment, then the earth will yield its fruits. In this way, we become partners with God, and really have an impact on the system of rewards and punishments. What does all this mean? Is the text just talking about fruits?

Develop a plan of action to insure that those who keep this *mitzvah* will indeed be rewarded.

My Mitzvah Action Plan

1. _____
2. _____
3. _____
4. _____
5. _____
6. _____
7. _____
8. _____
9. _____
10. _____

Now put it into action. Make it a Confirmation class project.

Personalizing the Principle of Faith

The personalization of this principle is very important, because it has the potential to direct our attention to our behavior and not really to concern ourselves with what others are doing or saying. How many times have you said to a parent, "It's just not fair. _____ (fill in any name) did it, and he/she did not get into trouble." And the familiar response, "Just worry about yourself, not other people," or something similar. It is difficult to try to follow specific *mitzvot* when others are not. Some people even say that the only purpose of this eleventh principle is to force people to behave. After all, if they are afraid of getting punished or if they are looking to be rewarded, then they will behave. That's the way things were when we were all young children. So, what happened? Do you or your friends live their lives that way? Or perhaps you do things because they are right, and avoid other things because they are wrong—and not because you may get into trouble if you are caught doing them. How do you make these kinds of difficult decisions in your life?

Rabbi Eugene Borowitz, perhaps the leading liberal Jewish theologian in the world, looks at it this way. He believes that Judaism is a set of behavioral ideals which we strive to reach. Though we may frequently fall short of our goal, we still strive to reach it. Taking a different perspective, Rabbi Harold Kushner, a well-known Conservative rabbi and author of the best-seller, *When Bad Things Happen to Good People*, argues that there is no system of rewards and punishment in the world. God set the world into motion, and then left us to work things out on our own. There are rules of nature. Sometimes things go haywire. They don't follow the pattern of nature that we expect them to follow, but they are nobody's fault. Sometimes, bad stuff just happens to good people! We turn to God for support and consolation, but God is not at fault, nor should we hold God responsible, says Rabbi Kushner.

Textual Encounters
Text 1:
> If you obey the commandments that I command you and serve God with all your heart and soul, then will I grant the rain for your land in season, the early rain and the later one.... Take care not to be lured away to serve other gods and bow to them. For God's anger will flare up against you, and God will shut up the skies so that there will be no rain and the ground will not yield its produce, and you will perish from off the good land ...
> (Deuteronomy 11:13–14, 16, 18)

Questions:

1. Do you believe that God rewards good behavior and punishes bad behavior? Do you have any evidence of this working in your own life or in someone else's life?

2. How do you explain the fact that sometimes a good person has a very difficult life or dies at an early age?

3. How might a person explain the text cited above in terms of ecology?

Text 2:

Because of our transgressions we were exiled from our land ...
"Holiness of the Day"
(Festival Musaf Amida)

Questions:

1. Do you believe that the various wanderings of the Jews throughout the centuries prior to the establishment of the Israelite nation were a result of the bad behavior of the Jewish people? How do you understand this verse from the *siddur*?

2. "The righteous shall flourish like the palm tree" (Psalm 92:13).

"Evildoers may spring up as the grass ... only to be destroyed forever" (Psalm 92:8).

In what way(s) do you believe that righteous people flourish? Are all evildoers eventually destroyed?

Text 3:

These are the only texts in the Torah in which *mitzvot* have rewards attached to them. Read them. Why do you think that the Torah chose these two *mitzvot* to be so important that specific rewards were attached to them? How do you interpret the meaning of the texts?

a. Honor your father and your mother, that you may long endure on the land that God is assigning to you. (Exodus 20:12)

b. If, along the road, you happen upon a bird's nest, in any tree or on the ground, with fledglings or eggs, and the mother sitting over the fledglings, do not take the mother together with the young. Let the mother go, and take only the young, in order that you may fare well and have a long life. (Deuteronomy 22:6)

Text 4:

Antigonus of Socho ... used to say, "Be not like servants who serve their master in the hope of receiving a reward. Rather, be like servants who serve their master with no expectation of receiving one."
(Pirke Avot 1:3)

Questions:

Why should a person do a good deed? Why is it better not to expect a reward for doing something good?

Text 5:

Ben He He said, "According to the suffering is the reward."
(Pirke Avot 5:26)

Question:

What do you think Ben He He meant by his remark?

Text 6:

These are the deeds that yield immediate reward and continue to do so in time to come: honoring parents; doing deeds of kindness; attending the house of study punctually; providing hospitality; visiting the sick; helping a needy bride; attending the dead; probing the meaning of prayer; and making peace between two persons. The study of Torah is the most basic of them all.
(Talmud, Shabbat 127a)

Questions:

What do all of these actions have in common? What does the text mean that in the doing of these things there will be continued reward in the future?

How Judaism Differs

While individual Jews, particularly liberal ones (and this includes all non-Orthodox Jews), don't like to talk about a system of reward and punishment (what is called divine retribution), this belief system has been in place as early as the rabbinic period. However, beliefs of this sort are really left to the individual, even though Maimonides was trying to set up a system of basic beliefs through these thirteen principles. As a matter of fact, such a principle fuels the controversy between those who argue that Judaism needs a set of basic principles of belief and those who argue that such beliefs should be left completely to the individual.

Protestant Christianity faces the same challenge. Although Christianity posits a similar system of divine retribution, liberal Protestants see this aspect of the world through the same prism in much the same way as do liberal Jews. However, because a belief in some type of heaven and hell forms more of the core of Christian belief, even liberal Christians tend to favor a belief in a system of reward and punishment. Salvation through the acceptance of Jesus as the Messiah is the way out of ultimate punishment. Since Christianity does not have a *mitzvah* system on which to base such rewards and punishment, it simply rewards good behavior and condemns sinful behavior as it is variously understood by individual denominations.

From Faith to Deeds

What can we as individuals do to make sure that the system works. Maimonides is talking about *mitzvot*. While we like to weigh all *mitzvot* equally, we believe that some are more important than others. But Maimonides (and Jewish tradition) does not make this distinction. If all *mitzvot* come from God, then all are to be equally followed. Any rejection of an individual *mitzvah* is a rejection of God.

Take two *mitzvot* that follow. Compare them. Consider their purpose, and the consequences of following them or not following them. How would you weight each *mitzvah*?

Even when we go astray, the rabbis have helped us to find a way back: *teshuva*, or repentance. We hear about it most during the High Holidays, but it is available to us all year long. Maimonides offered his own system for *teshuvah*. Here is what he said:

1. Make a confession before God:

by naming the sin;

voicing regret;

expressing shame;

and making a pledge not to do the sin again.

2. Then, abandon sin fully.

3. Change the way you think about the sin.

4. Change of name.

5. Make a contribution to charity.

6. Make supplication before God.

7. Make a public confession.

8. Acknowledge the sin you committed, on this Yom Kippur and next Yom Kippur.

9. Make amends and compensation to other people for the sin.

10. Apologize to the victim of the sin.

11. Then, exercise self-restraint by not repeating the sin the next time you have the opportunity.

Try using Maimonides' formula as part of your *teshuvah* process. Remember what the *machzor* teaches during Yom Kippur. Three things can avert the severity of a decree: *teshuvah*, *tzedakah*, and *tefillah*.

Godtalk

Mitzvot bring us closer to God. This is particularly true of ritual *mitzvot*. Some of us believe this is the primary purpose of ritual. Have you ever felt closer to God when following the performance of a particular ritual?

Describe it in the space below.

_____

_____

_____

_____

If the ritual you described was already part of your religious routine, what do you think made the ritual effective that particular time? How did you make it part of your religious routine?

On the other hand, sins drive us further from God. That's why some people believe that the sin necessarily includes its punishment. Thus, the system has its own inherent logic, and no one has to prove it through observing the world around us. What do you think of that idea?

What Can We Believe?

Reward and punishment. Are you prepared to accept the system of divine retribution that is advocated by Jewish tradition and affirmed by Maimonides? Or do you reject it as contrary to your experience of the world? Do you agree with the argument that *mitzvot* bring us closer to God, while sin drives us away from God? Or are you committed to search for the answer to this religious puzzle?

The Spectrum of Jewish Belief: Reform, Conservative, and All the Rest

Orthodox Judaism clearly believes that *mitzvot* were commanded by God. We have no choice but to follow these commandments, even those we do not fully understand. Because of our limitations as humans, we may not be able to comprehend the reason why God asked us to do these things. So we do them.

For Conservative Jews, a mitzvah is generally understood as an act performed in agreement with God's will. It includes the commandment and the law, the obligation to fulfill the law, as well as the act of fulfilling it. Since most Conservative Jews understand revelation as a two-way process, or a dialogue between God and humanity, the core of God's truth cannot be denied, but the ways in which people think about this truth as developed in the Bible and Talmud are subject to change and modification. Conservative Jews believe that the Bible and Jewish laws are the response of a community of people to God's call, and that *mitzvah* is human interpretation and application of divine principles. Within the Conservative movement, it is the task of the Committee of Law and Standards of the Rabbinical Assembly (the organizational union of Conservative rabbis) to decide upon modification of the law when it is deemed necessary.

Reform Jews like to translate the word *mitzvot* as "divine instructions" rather than as "commandments." Following the *mitzvot* has the potential to elevate our lives and make us holy. But not all of them make sense to us. Because Reform Jews do not feel the binding authority of *halakha*, they feel free to reject those *mitzvot* which no longer hold meaning for them or which may be contrary to their sense of what is right. This is particularly true with regard to equality between men and women and among the social classes. But this places a significant responsibility on each Reform Jew, who is required to evaluate each *mitzvah* as he or she considers its observance. With very few exceptions, the principle of personal autonomy does not give the individual the right to say, "Reform Jews do not do that." Instead, each Reform Jew must reason out each individual practice in dialogue with tradition, God, and one's conscience.

This complicates matters. If Reform Judaism argues that individuals have the right to accept or reject individual *mitzvot*, then one could not be punished for either following them or choosing not to. Classical Reform Judaism also rejected some of the ideas connected with the traditional view of the afterlife. Therefore, the notion of reward and punishment in the world-to-come does not seem to complement Reform Jewish ideology.

Reconstructionists believe that the system of *mitzvot* is important to the Jewish community. Therefore, they may feel free to reinterpret the reason behind the observance of a particular *mitzvah* before they reject it. While they do not see themselves as autonomous individuals, and do not permit themselves to reject any *mitzvot* on their own, they do exercise that right as a community.

No Jew fulfills all the *mitzvot*, and the number 613 may itself be considered an arbitrary enumeration. The key, as Rabbi Nachman of Bratslav teaches, is not merely the number of *mitzvot* one does, but the spirit in which one performs them.

PRINCIPLE TWELVE

The Messiah and the Messianic Age to Come

I believe with perfect faith in the coming of the Messiah, and, though Messiah tarry, I will wait daily for his coming.

Getting Started: Some Background

Do you remember the closing scenes from Fiddler on the Roof, the film adaptation of stories by Sholom Aleichem which feature Tevye and his daughters? Following a pogrom, the Jews of Anatevka realize that they must leave their beloved village. In the midst of their preparation to vacate their beloved village, the citizens ask their local rabbi, "We've waited thousands of years for the Messiah. Wouldn't this be a good time for him to come?" And the rabbi responds, "We'll just have to wait for him someplace else." This attitude of generally patient optimism permeates Jewish consciousness. References to the Messiah can be found throughout the prayer book. Although we have been waiting for a long time, never knowing when Messiah will come, we continue to wait. And while we wait, we work to bring the Messiah "soon, in our days." This is also the text that our people sang as they were forced into Nazi gas chambers.

But who or what is this Messiah, and what is supposed to happen when Messiah comes? The Messiah can be anyone, and can reveal himself (or, we would add, herself) at any time. It is a rabbinic tradition that the Messiah lives among beggars (and in former times, among the lepers). This is one of the reasons why we are to treat everyone warmly and with dignity. According to mainstream Jewish tradition, the Messiah will be a descendent of King David. This is an important idea to keep in mind as we consider what the Messiah will do. As was true of King David, the Messiah will arise as a political leader. Just as King David united the independent kingdoms of Israel and Judah, the Messiah will unite the Jewish community, and bring it to the Land of Israel. But the reach of the Messiah will not be limited to the Jewish community. Instead, the Messiah will redeem the whole world, thus ushering in the Messianic Age.

A Ready Reference

Messiah: In Hebrew, the word *mashiach*, "anointed one," is often combined with the Hebrew word for king. In the Bible, the term *mashiach* was originally used to refer to either an object or a person consecrated for a specific purpose. Eventually, it came to reflect the role of a designated person on a special mission from God. There are a variety of perspectives regarding the Messiah which have developed throughout the history of Jewish thought. Often, they gain centrality in Jewish thought. However, the Messiah is generally considered to be one who is a descendant in the line of King David, although there is also a prominent Josephan (or Ephraimitic) line for the Messiah in some areas of Jewish literature. Some scholars suggest that the Josephan Messiah will precede the Davidic Messiah, and will die in battle with the enemies of Israel. For some thinkers, the Josephan Messiah figures in the unification of the tribes of Israel as an important aspect of messianic doctrine. In any case, the Messiah is said to be a political-type leader who will bring the world to ultimate perfection. Such an individual will work for all, not just for those who believe in the possibility of redemption. Others believe that the Messiah will only come after humankind has brought the world to a level of human perfection on its own. Although there is a diversity of opinion as to how this might be accomplished, one source claims that it can be identified with the entire Jewish community celebrating and observing two Sabbaths in a row.

What We Believe

While thinkers differ on the details, the idea of a Messiah as someone who will save the Jewish people and direct them to their destiny has maintained a central role in Judaism. While we cannot find ideas of messianism in the Torah, most of the prophets articulate a vision of the Messiah. Most of the prophets envisioned messianism as part of a chain of events, which will begin with a severe judgment to be followed by a glorious future, at least, for a righteous remnant of the people. However, the messianism of the end of days (eschatology) is absent from the specific vocabulary of these prophets. Yet, the prophet known as Deutero-Isaiah is definitely eschatological in character (although still not in vocabulary). However, he too is not specific about a Davidic line. In the writings of Haggai and Zechariah, we find that the prophets expected the renewal of the Davidic kingdom by a specific individual. They thought that his presence would mark the new age, but not cause it.

The prophet is assigned the role of announcing the Messiah. As a result, Elijah emerges in various contexts in Jewish life. Make a list of the times in Jewish life when Elijah is called to mind. We will get you started.

1. At the end of the Havdalah ceremony, as a plea for him to come soon, in our days.

2. During Brit Milah, by placing the child in Elijah's chair.

3. In Eastern European heroic myths.

It is interesting to note that the editors of the Bible also made sure to emphasize the connection between Ruth, a Jew by choice, and King David, the forerunner of the Messiah. Why do you think the rabbis emphasized this point? Why did the rabbis not encourage Jewish proselytes? Do you think that Jews-by-choice feel differently about this idea than do those born into Judaism?

The rebuilding of the Temple became a central part of messianism after its destruction. Why do you think that the rebuilding of the Temple would be considered an important part of the messianic vision?

The Dead Sea Scrolls are a group of scrolls that was discovered near the Dead Sea in a series of caves in the ancient city of Qumran (in Israel, not too far from Masada). These scrolls are still being studied. As scholars evaluate them, they are learning a great deal about what has come to be know as the Dead Sea sect. (Some scholars identify this group as Essenes or as an early Judeo-Christian sect.) As is evidenced by the Dead Sea Scrolls, the Jews who lived in this community envisioned a pair of messiahs: a royal one from the house of David, and a priestly one from the descendants of Aaron. This gives rise to the consideration that maybe the anointed one was not to be a savior, as we might think. Instead, he was to be a socio-political figure. Some scholars who analyze this material suggest that the Dead Sea Scrolls reveal a belief in a tripartite Messiah, which includes the role of king, priest, and prophet. Christian scholars like to add that such an approach would prefigure the role of Jesus in Christianity.

Not everyone was content with waiting for the Messiah to appear and save the Jewish people. Some took the matter into their own hands—and failed. As a result of failed revolts, such as the Bar Kokhba rebellion (132–135 C.E.) and other similar messianic uprisings, Jewish thinkers emphasized the eschatology of messianism. This thereby excluded any other approach that emerged from experience of this world. While others saw Bar Kokhba as the Messiah, he referred to himself only as a *nasi*, or prince. Since Rabbi Akiva supported Bar Kokhba's revolt, presumably as an explicit messianic movement, we can assume that the rabbis promoted the idea that the messiah would be fully human. However, Akiva also declared that the Messiah would occupy a throne alongside God. In addition, at least one talmudic source ascribes immortality to the Messiah (see Talmud, Sukkah 52a). The change in attitude about Messianism transformed the suffering endured by such failures into a necessary prerequisite for the onset of *mashiach-zeit* (messiah time). It also meant that there could be no forcing of this time, encouraging only a "quiet waiting." This approach has long held sway over Jewish thought.

As might be expected, Maimonides argued for a rationalist approach to Messianism, one which posited a Messiah who was not a purveyor of miracles. He also opposed the messianic speculation of those like Abraham bar Chiyyah, who attempted, in his work called *Megillat ha-Megalleh*, to establish by astrological calculations the date of the coming of the Messiah. His contemporaries in the medieval world were preoccupied with trying to harmonize the often conflicting views in rabbinic literature. This is particularly important to note, since they did not receive a unified concept from the rabbis who preceded them. This discontinuity also helped to categorize the two salient areas of disagreement: a this-worldly Messianism (which focused on the ingathering of the dispersed, restoration of the Davidic kingdom, delivery from bondage, and rebuilding of the Temple) and an eschatological "end of days" Messianism (which focused on a day of judgment and resurrection of the dead). The most important contribution to this messianic literature is probably the Book of Zerubbabel, named for the last ruler of Judea from the Davidic line. He articulates a vision of the end of days and the time of the Messiah. According to this book, from among the literature named Pseudepigrapha (falsely ascribed works), the appearance of the Messiah will be preceded by the appearance of a satanic king of Rome. According to the author of the Book of Zerubbabel, this king is the son of Satan and a stone sculpture of a woman. The Josephan messiah will arise, and gather the Jews to Palestine and Jerusalem. But this ruler of Rome will slay him. Jerusalem will be saved by Hephzibah. Then, Hephzibah's son, from the Davidic line, will rise against the Roman king and kill him. Thus will the messianic age begin. This tale emerged out of the context of a strong Byzantine empire, as Heraclius, victorious against Persia, was about to conquer the world, and reunite the Eastern kingdom with Christianity. A vast literature emerged out of this apocalyptic tale. One of the most important is a book called *Otot Ha-Mashiach*, in which the author describes the ten events that are to take place before the coming of the Messiah. While the literature is rich in detail, little of it contains doctrinal or ideological elements. Likewise, while this literature describes the end of the world in detail, there is no hint as to why the end is to occur, and what the Jewish people might be able to do to hasten the redemption.

At the end of the *Aleynu* is a statement, "On that day, Adonai shall be One, and Adonai's name shall be one."

How is this a messianic statement? Why is it placed at the end of this prayer, which is near the end of every worship service? Why is this vision included in every worship service?

An Exercise

The political turmoil of the medieval period gave rise to a large body of messianic literature. Based on this history, try to analyze the political turmoil of the 1990s, and based upon this, determine what we might expect in the form of messianism. Begin by making a list of some of the great events of our time. We will get you started.

Reunification of Germany
Disintegration of the USSR
Recognition of Palestinian Autonomy

What else, do you think, should have to happen in the world before we might expect the Messiah?

Extending the Principle of Faith

Because we have been anxious to enter the messianic era, false Messiahs (also called pseudo-Messiahs) have arisen throughout Jewish history. How was it known that they were false?

Shabbetai Tzvi, who lived in the seventeenth century, was the best-known of the false Messiahs. His failure and its aftermath demoralized his followers. This cast a shadow on future messianic enthusiasm.

Here is the "litmus test" from the tradition for the qualities of the true Messiah:

1. A descendent of King David.
2. Gain sovereignty over the Land of Israel.
3. Gather the Jewish people from the four corners of the Earth.
4. Bring the Jewish people back to the Torah.
5. Bring peace to the whole world.

Make a list of criteria that you would impose should someone appear claiming to be the Messiah.

_____

_____

_____

_____

Do you see any signs in our time that the messianic age may be approaching?

Personalizing the Principle of Faith

Often we express a belief without realizing it. For example, consider the following song which you may sing in religious school or in your synagogue youth group. It even has some irrelevant hand motions and nonsense lyrics that go along with it. After reading the words or singing the song, consider its message. In the song, the two stages of Messianism are described. Stage 1 is a faith that the reign of David (which began in King David's time) would be eternal through a series of descendants to the throne. Stage 2 began after the death of Solomon with the collapse of the Davidic empire. Thus, people believed that an individual descendent of the House of David would arise and exercise dominion over the neighbors of Israel.

David melekh Yisrael, chai, chai, ve-kayam
Od avinu chai, od avinu chai.

Textual Encounters
Text I:

This is one of our favorite *midrashim* from the Talmud. It reflects both strands in Jewish thought about the coming of the Messiah. We have to wait, but we can also work to usher in the messianic age. What other conclusions can you draw from the story?

Rabbi Joshua came upon the prophet Elijah as he was standing at the entrance of the cave of Rabbi Simon bar Yochai. He asked him, "When is the Messiah coming?" The other answered, "Go and ask him yourself."

"Where shall I find him?" asked Rabbi Joshua. Came the reply, "Before the gates of Rome."

"And how shall I recognize him?" asked Rabbi Joshua. Elijah responded, "He will be sitting among the poor people covered with wounds. The others unbind their wounds all at once, and then bind them up again. But he unbinds them, one wound at a time, and then rebinds them immediately. He says to himself, 'If I am needed—I must be ready to go and not be late.'"

So Rabbi Joshua went to the gates of Rome and found him. "Peace be with you, my master and teacher." He answered, "And peace be with you, son of Levi."

Rabbi Joshua continued, "When are you coming, master?" Thereupon he answered, "Today."

Then, Rabbi Joshua returned to Elijah, and said to him, "He has deceived me. He told me that he would come today, but he has not come."

But Elijah responded, "This is what he told you: 'Today, if you would hearken to God's voice!'" (Psalm 95:7).

(Talmud, Sanhedrin 98a)

The philosopher and theologian Martin Buber once recalled his grandfather teaching this text to him when he was a young child. After he heard the story, the young Buber inquired: "Grandfather! What is he waiting for?" The grandfather replied, "My child, he is waiting for you."

Text 2:

If you are in the process of planting a sapling and the Messiah arrives, finish your planting and, then go out to greet the Messiah.
(Avot de-Rabbi Natan 31b)

Why would Jewish tradition and the rabbis make this suggestion? Have you ever been in the middle of doing something important, but had to stop to do something that was also important? How do you make your decision regarding what to finish first?

Text 3:

Maimonides concludes the section on the Messiah in his code of Jewish law with the following statement:

At that time, there will be neither hunger nor war, neither envy nor competition, for good will be found in great abundance, and all delicacies as accessible as the dust of the earth. The whole world will have no occupation other than to know Adonai. Consequently, Israel will be great sages, knowing undisclosed matters, and grasping knowledge of their Creator insofar as this lies within human power. As it is said, 'For the earth shall be full of the knowledge of Adonai, as the waters cover the sea' (Isaiah 11:9).
(*Mishneh Torah, Hilchot Melakhim* 12:5)

How would you conclude a discussion on messianism? What text would you use to illustrate your statement? Why do you think that Maimonides chose this text from the writings of the prophet Isaiah?

Text 4:

Here is a series of texts. Choose one that represents your conception of messianism, and claim it as your own. Remember to be prepared to explain its meaning, and why you relate so personally to it. All of the statements are from the Talmud, Sanhedrin 98a–b.

The son of David will not come until the generation that will be either all righteous or all wicked.

The son of David will not arrive until all qualities are equal in all human beings.

Rabbi Zeiri said, in Rabbi Chanina's name: The son of David will not come until there are no conceited people in Israel.

The son of David will not come until all the arrogant cease from Israel.

Rabbi Yochanan said, "Wait for the Messiah. When you see generations of Israel diminishing and many troubles coming upon them, then the Messiah will appear.

Rabbi Nachman said, "If he (the Messiah) is of those living today, it might be a person like myself, as it is written 'And their nobles shall be of themselves, and their governors shall proceed from the midst of them' (Jeremiah 30:21)."

How Judaism Differs

While the Christian concept of the Messiah emerges out of the Jewish idea of messianism, the approach to the subject in the two faith communities developed independently over time. As a result, there is a marked distinction among contemporary Jews and Christians. However, the basic thrust remains the same. Messianism is a somewhat private affair. In traditional Judaism the coming of the Messiah is a widely accepted belief. For many liberal Jews it is a matter of personal conscience. For Jews, the advent of the Messiah and messianic times affects the entire world.

Compare the two approaches below:

Jewish

Christian

From Faith to Deeds

Why is it that there are those who have the right to vote but choose not to? Some argue that their vote is of no consequence, particularly in the American presidential election, which is decided through the electoral college system. And in Israel, which has a very high voter turnout (some statistics suggest over 95 percent), the last election was the first in which citizens elected a prime minister, rather than having the election of the prime minister determined by individual political parties. In previous elections, citizens voted for parties. The more votes a party received determined the number of Knesset seats to be held by that party. And the party that received the greatest number of votes had the right to place the prime minister in office (as head of that party). This changed with the election of Benjamin Netanyahu as prime minister (who defeated Shimon Peres). Beginning with that election, people voted for their parties; parties developed lists of party members who would hold Knesset seats, the number of which was determined by the number of votes garnered in the election. And separately, people voted for the prime minister. The prime minister's obligation was then to form a coalition of parties (through members of the Knesset) in order to run the government.

Some people believe that their vote does not matter. Likewise, there are those who think that they can do nothing to usher in the messianic age. And that what they do will have no impact on preventing it, as well. Think about your life over the past six months. What can you identify that has either helped to move us closer to the Messianic age or moved us further away from it?

Toward the Messiah:

_____

_____

_____

_____

_____

Keeping the Messiah Away:

_____

_____

_____

_____

_____

Now, plan your activities for the next six months. What will you avoid? What will you do to help bring the Messiah into our midst?

Godtalk

If the prayer book reflects the ongoing dialogue between God and the Jewish people throughout history, then we should be able to find transcripts of the conversation about the Messiah. So take a look at the Amidah, and see what you can find about the Messiah. Write the pertinent texts below, and determine what relationship they may have to your life. (Hint: There may be a difference in these statements in the Reform, Reconstructionist, and Conservative prayer books.)

Our Talk

Complete the following sentences:

I believe that the Messiah is_____.

I believe that the Messiah will come when_____.

I believe that the Messiah will do the following:_____.

While the topic of the Messiah is serious, there are aspects of the conversation that are neither so serious nor so literal. For example, there is a wonderful Yiddish folksong that asks, "What will be when the Messiah comes?" Drawing on a variety of rabbinic imaginings, it tells of a great banquet that will be held for the righteous. At this banquet, the meat of the Leviathan and the Behemot (two mythic creatures) will be served, as well as wine that has been stored in the vat "from the six days of creation." Moses will teach Torah at the banquet. Miriam will dance. And King David will recite *birkat ha-mazon* (grace after meals). What do these elements represent? Remember that the goal of the writer is to suggest that everything will be more perfect than the present.

The Spectrum of Jewish Belief: Reform, Conservative, and All the Rest

The Reform movement rejected the notion of a single Messiah who brings the world to the ultimate goal of perfection. Instead, Reform thinkers, along with Reconstructionists, write about the messianic era as a time in which all will contribute to the fulfillment of human potential. Thus, rather than considering that the Messiah may be anyone, Reform thinkers have rephrased that notion, and suggested that the Messiah may be in anyone. In other words, we all have messianic potential. We are all capable of helping to make real the messianic era. This also means that the Messiah need not be a descendent of King David. Reconstructionism likewise rejects the notion of a personal Messiah. However, Mordecai Kaplan, founder of the Reconstructionist movement, wrote in 1956, in *Questions Jews Ask*, "We can no longer believe that any person or semidivine being, is divinely destined to rule as the Messiah, and usher in the millennium. Nevertheless, the idea of a Messiah can still figure symbolically to express the valid belief in the coming of a higher type of man [sic] than this world has yet known."

Reform Judaism also disassociated the belief in messianism with any return to Zion. The destruction of the Temple and the exile of the Jewish people is not seen as a punishment. Rather, it is considered an opportunity to spread ethical monotheism to the four corners of the Earth. This changed, however, with Reform's official embrace of Zionism in the Columbus Platform of 1937.

Conservative Judaism affirms a period of Messianism without supernatural intervention.

Post-Enlightenment secularism identified Messianism with the goals of social and political tolerance with full emancipation (and the diminution of nationalist ideals). Religious Zionism has undergone an ideological change in its approach to messianism with the establishment of the State of Israel as "the beginning of the sprouting of our redemption."

Chabad (Lubavich) has attracted a great deal of attention over the past several years with the expectations of many of its followers of the imminent advent of the Messiah in the form of their rebbe.

Traditional (Orthodox) Judaism, in general, maintains the classic rabbinic doctrine. The Messiah will be a descendent of the House of David. He will rule in Jerusalem, rebuild the temple, and reestablish the sacrificial system. While there are some Orthodox rabbis who oppose Zionism, most view the establishment of the State of Israel as the beginning of our redemption, as the foundation laid by humans to usher in the messianic era.

PRINCIPLE THIRTEEN

Life, Death, and Beyond

I believe with perfect faith that there will be a resurrection of the dead at the time when it shall please the Creator, praised be Your name, and exalted be the remembrance of You for ever and ever.

Getting Started: Some Background

The doctrine of *tichiyat ha-metim* (resurrection of the dead) is probably a result of the influence of the ancient Persian religion of Zoroastrianism on Judaism. It is a belief that the dead will live again at some future time when they will be reunited with their physical bodies and thereby participate in the triumph of a messianic rule on earth. According to some accounts, the individual must wait until this time in a place identified as *Sheol*, which was often pictured in a variety of unpleasant ways. The idea of *Sheol* originated in the late biblical period, and remains critical to the Jewish view of an afterlife. The concept of physical resurrection was a central tenet of rabbinic Judaism. The notion of resurrection implied that the Israelite nation would be redeemed, that a divinely inspired social order would be formed, and that there would be divine retribution for the righteous. With the Book of Daniel we learn that the righteous will be judged along with the wicked. According to Saadia Gaon, there will be two periods of resurrection: one during the messianic era, and the second in the world-to-come.

While the details of resurrection were debated among Jewish thinkers since the rabbinic period, one thing is clear: The rabbinic notion of resurrection focused on a physical resurrection of the body, and was not limited to the spiritual resurrection of the soul.

A Ready Reference

These are terms that are associated with the idea of resurrection. Become familiar with them. You may find some of them on your S.A.T.

Day of YHWH: The day when Israel's foes will be conquered, and a new era will dawn, during which time the nation of Israel will enjoy material prosperity.

End of Days: This period of time (*acharit ha-yamim*), which is distinct from the afterlife of the individual, signals the beginning of the messianic era. It is the end of recorded history, as we know it.

Gan Eden: Using the same term to refer to the original paradise in which Adam and Eve originally frolicked, *Gan Eden* is the place where righteous souls dwell. Within the ethical constructs of rabbinic Judaism, *Gan Eden* and *Gehenna* are diametrically opposed to each other. Yet, the rabbis also considered this place to be posthistorical, i.e., it will "evolve" after the unfolding of regular history and the beginning of the reign of the Messiah. In this paradise, all of the "inhabitants" will live in the presence of God (or, at least, the *Shechina*). This place of paradise is also often the place in which the treasury of souls (*otzar neshamot*) is located. Sometimes this treasury is associated with the term *tzror ha-chayim* (the bonds of eternal life), or a reservoir of souls from whence all souls derive, and to which all souls return after the bodily death of the individual in whose body the soul is housed. According to Nachmanides, *Gan Eden* is the place of reward where the righteous wait for the (collective) world-to-come following their individual corporeal deaths.

Gehenna: Sometimes called *Gehinnom*, according to the First

Book of Enoch, *Gehenna* is hell, simply, a place of eternal damnation. Yet, the rabbis make more of it. They call it by a variety of names, and even equate it with *Sheol*. One thing is clear. This is the realm of punishment after death. It is, therefore, part of the ethical view of the world as through the prism of the rabbis. The threat of *Gehenna* motivated the average Jew to live an ethical life, guided by God's *mitzvot*. For Nachmanides, *Gehenna* is not a place of equal punishment. Each individual's *Gehenna* is different than that of another persons, and this is determined by his or her (mis)deeds and the consequent divine punishment. It is the place the soul enters after death. Here, the soul—not the body—is subjected to punishment.

Soul: By most accounts, the soul existed prior to its entrance into the body, and lives beyond the death of the body. Thus, the notion of immortality is an integral part of any eschatological understanding of life and death. This basic understanding was transformed by the medieval philosophers, as they attempted to integrate rabbinic notions of immortality with the philosophers' newfound understanding of the essence of the soul. The philosophers were more interested in the metaphysical understanding of immortality and less interested in the mythic descriptions that colored rabbinic literature. For Saadia Gaon, for example, the soul can be polished through righteous actions. The fires of *Gehenna*, on the other hand, are used to purge the tarnish of the wicked soul. He believed that the soul was created at the same time as the body. It is at that time that God's presence is manifest, and thus the soul becomes immortal. For Saadia, the soul is made of a material similar to the heavenly spheres. It is luminescent because of the divine light cast on it generated by God.

World-to-come: The notion of a world-to-come (*olam ha-ba*) was born during the period of rabbinic Judaism, and became one of the two pivotal notions by which the rabbis wrestled communal authority away from the priestly ruling class. The Talmud puts it this way: "In the world-to-come, there is no eating, drinking, washing, anointing, or sexual intercourse, but the righteous sit with their crowns on their heads enjoying the radiance of the Shechina" (Talmud, Berakhot 17a). The world-to-come is a reference used frequently in the Talmud and Midrash to the future life after death. Often, it is used in juxtaposition to *olam ha-zeh* (this world). Thus, if this world exists on a physical plane, then the world-to-come (or the next world, as it is also called) exists on a purely spiritual plane. This is not to say that the world-to-come is superior to this world. As a matter of fact, the rabbis suggest the opposite: "Better is one hour of repentance and good works in this world than a whole life in the world-to-come" (Pirke Avot 4:22). Nevertheless, the same sages wrote: "Better is one hour of bliss in the world-to-come than the whole of life in this world" (Pirke Avot 4:22).

What We Believe

Each individual is part of the mind-body continuum in the Jewish understanding of life; so too is the world. Thus, both this world and the next world are important. However, most rabbis will argue that the focus of Judaism remains on this life. Yet, since both the body and the soul are important, they should not be considered as separate entities. Perhaps the early rabbis intentionally sought this tension to motivate the individual to do good works in this world. Or, maybe, they were trying to deal with the reality of the world that surrounded them, just as we try to work out problems in the world in which we live. Nevertheless, the rabbis also expressed this notion as reflecting a utopian, messianic era which is manifest in society. The messianic era, which we learned about in the previous chapter, will, therefore, be characterized by righteousness, social justice, and material prosperity for all who deserve it. And bodily resurrection is just a part of that world construct.

Jews and Judaism have generally been more concerned with this world than the next, and have concentrated their religious efforts toward building an ideal world for the living. The following describes most of the forms in which our people conceive of immortality today:

1. Immortality through family. We live on through the life of our family and their descendants. This is another way of saying that we live in and through our children. This naturalistic view says that eternal life occurs biologically through the children we bring into the world.

2. Immortality through influence. When we have influenced others to the point that they fashion themselves after us and continue to use us as a role model, this kind of eternal significance is itself a form of immortality.

3. Immortality through deeds and creative works. Our work can outlast our life, however modest. We will continue to live through our work. This notion of immortality is expressed in the Midrash: "We need not erect monuments to the righteous; their deeds are their monuments" (Genesis Rabbah 32:10).

4. Immortality through memory. People live on in the memories of those who knew and loved them. Simply remembering people who we admired and loved gives them eternity.

5. Reincarnation. The kabbalists, the medieval Jewish mystics, proposed still another option. They taught that a person's soul returns again and again in different bodies, and the way in which it conducts itself in each incarnation determines its ascent or descent in its next visit.

6. Resurrection. Many Jews in the past believed that the physical body would be resurrected during the messianic era. Some still hold this view today.

7. Eternal life. The deceased live with God, and will be restored to their bodies when the Messiah appears.

8. Rationalist view. Maimonides proposed, in contrast to the mystics, that, in as much as God is pure intelligence, one's godlike qualities reside in the intellect. Therefore, to the extent that we develop our intelligence and reach the knowledge of eternal truth, we achieve immortality.

An Exercise

This exercise does not require a lot of writing. Instead, it demands a lot of reflective thought. What do you think happens when you die? Does what you think offer you a measure of comfort in thinking about the death, God forbid, of those you love or in thinking about the trajectory of your own life? Think it through completely. Then, write your thoughts below.

_____

_____

_____

_____

_____

_____

_____

_____

Extending the Principle of Faith

While the notion of reincarnation is not part of mainstream Judaism, it does occupy a prominent role in the history of Jewish thought. The idea is called _gilgul ha-nefesh_, literally, a rolling over of souls. The idea works something like this: As part of your work in _teshuva_, you are given the opportunity to do better in your next life. However, that opportunity is not given to you if you are not prepared to use it as a means of _teshuva_.

While some people are not prepared to talk about reincarnation, they do recognize that things happen in life that are difficult to explain. Rabbi Shira Millgrom likes to call them windows, because they offer us a glimpse of the world beyond. (For some, that is what the peacefulness of Shabbat is all about—a foretaste of the world-to-come.)

Have you ever experienced being somewhere or doing something, feeling as if you had been there before or done it before? How do you explain it? Record the incident below.

_____

_____

Personalizing the Principle of Faith

Unlike the other principles, which Maimonides writes extensively about in their original contexts, he says nothing about this principle. Even Hasdai Crescas did not call it a fundamental principle. Instead, he referred to it as a fundamental belief. Perhaps both philosophers were uncomfortable with the idea. Or maybe they felt that belief in such an idea was highly personal, and wanted to leave it totally up to the individual.

What do you think? Should Judaism mandate these principles? Is it possible to do so? When Confirmation was introduced to Judaism, synagogues required a form of catechism, that is, the repetition of formalized doctrinal statements, which students were asked to publicly *confirm*. Does repeating something over and over force it into your psyche, make it part of your spiritual self?

Try repeating this principle over and over. Recast it into different forms (audio or video recording, write it down, etc.). Does it make a difference?

Textual Encounter:

Here is the prophet Amos' description of the Day of YHWH:
According to the prophet Amos,

A time is coming, declares Adonai, when the plowman shall meet the reaper, and the treader of grapes, him who holds the seed; when the mountains shall drip sweet wine, and all the hills shall wave (with grain).... And they shall plant vineyards, and drink their wine; they shall till gardens, and eat their fruit.
(Amos 9:13–14)

After you have read Amos' words, put his description in your own words. What do you think he is attempting to describe? How would you describe the same vision?

Isaiah saw it another way,

In the days to come, the mountain of YHWH's house shall be established above the mountains and tower over the hills; and all the nations shall gaze on it with joy, and the many peoples shall go, and say, "Come let us go up to the mountain of YHWH to the house of the God of Jacob; that God may instruct us in divine ways, and we may walk in God's paths." For Torah shall come forth from Zion, the word of Adonai from Jerusalem".
(Isaiah 2:2–3).

How does Isaiah's vision compare to the vision of Amos?

Below is a selection from the Mishnah that includes a passage from Isaiah concerning who will have a place in the world-to-come. After you have read the Mishnah's requirements, develop your own list of criteria.

All Israelites have a share in the world-to-come (Rabbi Neil Gillman likes to translate this as the "age-to-come") as it is said, "Your people also shall all be righteous, they shall inherit the land forever; the branch of my planting, the work of my hands, that I may be glorified."
(Isaiah 60:21).

And these are the ones who have no portion in the world-to-come. The one who says that the resurrection of the dead is a teaching that does not derive from the Torah, and that the Torah does not come from heaven, and an Epicurean.
(Mishnah, Sanhedrin 10:1)

With the exception of Pirke Avot, the Mishnah seldom deals explicitly with issues of belief. Why do you think that the rabbis decided to include this principle, as did Maimonides?

If the body was to be resurrected, then the rabbis had to consider the process by which this would be accomplished. Thus, they considered the physical anatomy of the human, and determined how resurrection would take place. This is what one rabbi concluded:

Hadrian (the Roman emperor), may his bones be crushed, asked Rabbi Joshua ben Hananiah, "From which part of the body will the Holy Blessed One, in the time-to-come, cause the human to sprout forth?" He answered, from the nut (in Hebrew, luz) of the spinal column (probably referring to the tip of the coccyx). Said Hadrian, "How can you convince me?" He then brought one before him. He put it in water, but it was not dissolved. He let it pass through millstones, but it was not ground. He put it in fire, but it was not burnt. He put it on an anvil, and began beating it with a hammer, but the anvil was flattened out, and the hammer was split, but all this had no effect.

(Leviticus Rabbah 18:1)

The classic vision of resurrection comes from the prophet Ezekiel, and it is called the "dry bones" vision. In it the prophet sees a skeleton regaining its flesh and organs through the spirit of God. Read through Ezekiel 37 with your classmates. Use the classic rabbinic approach to interpretation to understand the text. Remember the approach through the acronym (pardes—for paradise, which in itself contains a variety of meanings). Consider the text on its simplest level, what is called the peshat. Next, take a look at the text for its remez, any hints (or insights) that the texts may be offering to the reader. Then, consider the derash, the interpretative elements in the text. Finally, look for a sod, a secret that the text may be trying to reveal.

In the midrash to Psalms (118:20)

"Open the gates of righteousness." When a person is asked in the world-to-come, "What is your work?" and that person answers, "I feed the hungry," all will be well for that person. "This is the gate of Adonai" (Psalm 118:20). Enter into it, you who feed the hungry. And when a person answers, "I give drink to the thirsty," all will be well for that person. "This is the gate of Adonai" (Psalm 118:20). Enter into it, you who gives drink to the thirsty. And when a person answers, "I clothe the naked," all will be well for that person. "This is the gate of Adonai" (Psalm 118:20). Enter into it, you who clothe the naked. This will also be said to the one who helps raise the orphan, to those who give tzedakah, or performed loving deeds of kindness.

Now, ask yourself the question: How am I living my life? What did I do today to make life better for someone else?

How Judaism Differs

The Christian idea of bodily resurrection, which is evident in the central focus of Christianity (i.e., the resurrection of Jesus as the Christ), emerges from this rabbinic notion. However, some Christians see this as a spiritual resurrection rather than a physical one.

From Faith to Deeds

How does one actualize a belief in bodily resurrection? Even for those who don't focus their attention on this idea, it infiltrates routine, daily liturgy. Consider the following from the morning blessings. It has been set to music by the Jewish folksinger Debbie Friedman:

> My God, the soul that You have given me is pure. You created it. You fashioned it. You breathed it into me. You safeguarded it in me, and You will eventually take it from me, and return it to me in the time to come. As long as the soul is within me, I thank You Adonai, my God, and God of my ancestors, Master of all things, Guide of all souls. Praised are You, Adonai, who restores souls to dead bodies.

The brief version, to be said upon waking:

Modeh ani. I thank You, living and eternal Ruler, for having restored my soul within me with compassion—abundant is Your faithfulness.

And here is a text taken from the second benediction of the Amida:

God keeps faith with those who sleep in the dust, and will, according to God's mercy, raise the dead, restore them bodily, and grant them eternal life.

Find the entire paragraph in your synagogue's prayer book. Does the context change the meaning at all?

Godtalk

As Rabbi Neil Gillman, who may be called the foremost contemporary Conservative theologian, once said to us, "If God is so powerful, then why can't God raise the body after you are dead? That would put an end to death." What do you think?

What Can We Believe?

Some people think that we should talk about these ideas more. Some of them even think that we should use the ideas when we counsel those who have suffered a loss through death of one whom they love, or even if they are anticipating their own death. In other words, if people were to believe in an afterlife that included bodily resurrection, maybe they would not be so anxious about death.

Those who accept the concept of bodily resurrection believe that eternal life in the presence of God is immensely pleasurable, and a result of unmerited generosity. Those who affirm it also seek it. Perhaps it is a meaningful concept only for those who long for such a relationship. And if one thirsts for an intimate relationship with God in this life (which is limited by time), why wouldn't that same person want to pursue such a relationship after death (which is unlimited by time)?

Here is what Maimonides said about the idea elsewhere, in an piece he called "Essay on Resurrection":

> It is not rare that a person aims to expound the intent of some conclusions clearly and explicitly, makes an effort to reject doubts and eliminate far-fetched interpretations, and yet the unbalanced will draw the reverse judgment of the conclusions the individual sought to clarify. Some such thing occurred even to one of God's declarations... If this is what happened to God's proclamations, it is much more likely to be expected to happen to statements by humans. _____

_____

_____

_____

_____

_____

But not everyone agreed with him. The thirteenth-century mystic Meshullam ben Solomon da Piera (also known as En Vidas de Gerona), said, "I will believe in resurrection, when the body and soul will arise and the bones will come to life again." But the question remains, if people are uncomfortable with the idea, then why does it endure as part of the belief system?

The Spectrum of Jewish Belief: Reform, Conservative, and All the Rest

In the case of belief in resurrection, it is probably better to look at the issue historically within the movements, rather than compare it within the context of one movement or another. For the most part, the issue of physical resurrection receded from the center of Jewish thought following the medieval period, although it remained one of the "official" tenets of rabbinic Judaism. In the medieval period, we see that even Maimonides was uncomfortable with the idea. The classical reformers rejected the notion entirely, in favor of a spiritual resurrection (of the soul), which the posture of Maimonides clearly welcomes. However, today, we are experiencing what Rabbi Neil Gillman described as the postmodern impulse. This idea of postmodernism is characterized, according to Rabbi Eugene B. Borowitz, the leading liberal Jewish theologian, as "an intuition seeking self-understanding." Gillman goes further; he contends that ideas like resurrection have the potential to "reenchant" the world. The bottom line seems to be that most Reform Jews do not accept the idea. However, some have reintroduced the idea into the liturgy, intrigued, like other members of this generation, by the notion of a physical, as well as spiritual, resurrection.

For Conservative Jews, death does not mean extinction. Many Conservative Jews affirm and understand literally the traditional doctrine of bodily resurrection of the dead and the continued existence, after death and through eternity, of the individual soul. Others understand this teaching in a more figurative way: One's identity and ability to touch people and society does not end with the physical death of one's body. Great personalities from the beginning of history continue to remain potent influences in the world.

Reconstructionist Jews historically rejected the idea, but did not remove it from the liturgy because of its poetic power. However, its theology is undergoing a great deal of change and evolution.

Orthodoxy continues to accept the idea of bodily resurrection. However, its thinkers differ on the specific events that will take place during the time of the Messiah.

Shavuot: Seeing Ourselves as the Reflected Light of Torah

When Moses went up Mount Sinai to speak to God, the Israelites waited for him to return. They were so very anxious, because they wondered what God would say to Moses. When they saw Moses coming down from the mountain, they noticed that he seemed disappointed, and asked him why. Moses answered, "God wants to make an agreement with us, and give us a precious gift as a sign of that agreement."

Excitedly, the people asked, "What is the gift?"

Said Moses, "It is called the Torah. The light of truth shines in its words like pearls in the dark seas. Stories which teach us how God wants us to live are contained in the Torah. There are also laws that will teach us how to live as free people, so that we will never know slavery in our hearts again."

The people remembered Egypt and their enslavement. They didn't want to return to slavery; they yearned to be free. They wanted to live with inner peace. They thought, "God's Torah truly is a great gift."

Moses added, "God will not give us the gift of Torah unless we promise God something in return. We must offer God some form of collateral."

Then, the people understood Moses' disappointment. They too became saddened. "What do we have to offer God as collateral? A gift like this is worth empires. But we are poor and live in the desert. We will never have the gift of Torah."

The women offered their bracelets with rubies and rings with diamonds to give to God in exchange for the Torah. So Moses went up the mountain again, and returned, but he was still sad.

"God has said that the Torah is more precious than all the diamonds in the world. The Torah is so bright that it will light up the souls of the entire people. Not even a thousand diamonds will do that."

The people sat on the desert sands, and reflected on Moses' words throughout the night. When the sun finally came up, they had an idea. "We will offer our great leaders Moses and Aaron to God as collateral for the Torah. Surely God knows the loyalty of these two great leaders."

So Moses went up the mountain again, but again he returned with a look of disappointment. "God has spoken," he said, "and told me that Aaron and I are unacceptable as collateral. We have already pledged our loyalty to God. There is nothing more that we can give God."

In the camp of the Israelites was an old woman whose wisdom was great. When she heard what Moses said, she addressed the people. "We have been offered God's most precious possession, the Torah. In return, we must offer God *our* most precious possession. If a person would choose only one thing in the world to possess, would one choose precious jewels? No. Would one choose money? No. Then what would one choose, if one is given only one choice? The answer is clear: one's children."

Hearing the wisdom in the old woman's words, the people turned to Moses, and said, "We will offer our children as collateral for the Torah. If God will give us the Torah, we will teach it faithfully to our children. And our children will teach it to their children."

So Moses went back up the mountain to speak to God. When he came down it was Shavuot. With him were the two tablets of the

Law. He stood before the Israelites, and said, "God has said that all people are God's children, and the children of humanity are indeed precious to God. They are worthy collateral for the gift of the Torah."

The Israelites thanked God by keeping God's commandments, by studying God's Torah, and teaching that Torah to their children, from that day unto this one.

You, the Confirmation students, are that precious collateral which the people promised God. In each one of you is the reflected light of Torah. As confirmands, you will stand in your synagogue on Shavuot (the day that God gave Torah to our people) to affirm that the echo from Sinai can still be heard, that the agreement our ancestors made is still binding.

Confirmation is not about graduation. You are not now free from obligation. You have the responsibility to engage the Torah. It is your study that transforms the text into Torah. And in doing so, you too can be transformed. Enter the pages of the text. Drink from its redemptive waters. Find inner peace within its pages.

You will come to Shavuot with the first fruits of your labors as adult Jews. What are those fruits? You have continued your Jewish education beyond the time when you became B'nai and B'not Mitzvah. And you have come to reaffirm your commitment to Judaism and the Jewish people, the commitment you first considered when you became Bar or Bat Mitzvah.

Some people think that Shavuot is a holiday that is celebrated each spring for two days (generally one day among Reform, Reconstructionist, and Israeli Jews—a result of a difference in calendrical approaches). Two days, and it is over. But, like the rest of the Jewish holiday calendar, although a particular date may highlight one aspect of the Jewish experience, images of the holiday are reflected throughout the year. The giving of Torah is celebrated on Shavuot, but the receiving of Torah is celebrated and simulated each time we publicly read the Torah in the midst of our community.

In many Sephardic congregations, there is a wonderful custom which takes place prior to the Torah reading on the first day of Shavuot. A *ketubah le-Shavuot* (a marriage certificate for Shavuot) is read; a symbol of the relationship between God and the Jewish people. It may sound strange, but we have a relationship with God—which is similar in many ways to marriage. The Torah itself is a love letter, sent by God to the Jewish people. That's why we treat it the way we do. We kiss and caress it. We look for meaning in every stroke of the scribal pen, in every nuance of expression, in every word, of the text. We are constantly searching for God's love as we immerse ourselves in the text.

It is our hope that you will continue to as a partner with God, to remember what happened at Sinai, and to rekindle the flames of love through devotion to God and Judaism.

This is the threefold promise of the bride and groom, taken from the writings of the prophet Hosea (2:21–22), which is often repeated by students during their service of confirmation. We invite you to do the same:

> I will betroth you forever, and I will betroth you and make you mine through righteousness and justice, through lovingkindness, mercy, and faithfulness. And I shall be devoted to God.

We wish you and your entire Confirmation class a hearty mazal tov upon your wonderful achievement. And may you continue to grow in spirit and in strength.

B'vracha,

Rabbi Ron Isaacs
Rabbi Kerry Olitzky

Getting Ready for Confirmation

In preparation for your Confirmation, it's time to develop your own set of basic Jewish principles. Here is an example of how one rabbi reframed the principles, just to help get you started.

I believe in the power of faith to bring sanctity and dignity to the lives of humans, to transform them into conscious children of God.

I believe in the reality of the living God, who while transcending time and space, dwells and works in all things at all times. God is the Source of all being, and the Parent and Master of all humans.

I believe that God reveals the divine self in the cosmic order and in the life, mind, and spirit of humankind.

I believe that God's revelation to the prophets of Israel and of other peoples offers a light for all people in their spiritual and moral striving.

I believe it is Israel's mission to continue to witness to God before all people.

I believe in the sanctity of human life, in the perfectibility of human character, and in the deathlessness of the human soul.

I believe in the human potential to range oneself on the side of God, to free oneself from sin, weakness, and brutality, and to overcome the obstacles that impede one's moral and spiritual growth.

I believe in the possibility of ushering in the reign of peace on earth, in the triumph of good over evil, in the banishment of war, and in the establishment of peace in the hearts of humans and nations.

Rabbi Samuel S. Cohon,
Essays in Jewish Theology (adapted)

Now, write out each principle to reflect your personal beliefs about the subject. You can use the introductory phrase that Maimonides chose or one of your own.

1. _____

_____

2. _____

_____

3. _____

_____

4. _____

_____

5. _____

_____

6. _____

_____

7. _____

_____

8. _____

_____

9. _____

_____

10. _____

_____

11. _____

_____

12. _____

_____

13. _____

_____

Yigdal

People express themselves in a variety of ways. Often, difficult theological concepts are turned into verse. And verse is turned into song. Yigdal is a poetic rendition of Maimonides' Thirteen Principles, commonly sung at the conclusion of Friday evening worship services. The Sephardic version includes this fourteenth line: "These are the thirteen bases of the Jewish faith and the tenets of God's law. Let God's holy name be worshiped and praised for ever." Other songs of this kind were written in the same period, but this is the only one that found its way into the liturgy. It is attributed to Daniel ben Judah, a judge in Rome in the first half of the fourteenth century. It is also ascribed to Immanuel (ben Solomon) of Rome.

There is a Creator who alone created and creates all things. God is one, unique. God has no body, no form. God is eternal. God alone is to be worshiped. The words of the prophets are true. Moses was the greatest of the prophets. The source of the Torah is divine. The Torah is immutable. God knows the deeds and the thoughts of humans. God rewards and punishes. The Messiah will come. God, forever praised, will resurrect the dead.